YOU NEXT

A STEP-BY-STEP GUIDE TO TAKING CHARGE OF YOUR CAREER

Mary C. Kelly, PHD

Meridith Elliott Powell, MBA

You Next
A Step-By-Step Guide To Taking Charge Of Your Career

© 2025 Mary C. Kelly and Meridith Elliott Powell.
All rights reserved.

Published by:
Productive Leaders
420 Lena Lane
Franklin, TN 37067

No part of this book may be reproduced or transmitted in any form or by any means, electronic or mechanical, including but not limited to: photocopying, recording, or by any information storage retrieval system without the written permission of the publisher, except for the inclusion of brief quotations in a review.

Printed in the United States of America.

Cover Design and Interior Layout: Oprah Milan

Print: ISBN: 978-1-935733-39-3
Kindle ISBN: 978-1-935733-40-9

Mary C. Kelly
www.ProductiveLeaders.com
mary@productiveleaders.com

Meridith Elliott Powell
www.MeridithElliottPowell.com
mere@valuespeaker.com

TABLE OF CONTENTS

Acknowledgements vii

Introduction ix

    1. Where Are You Now? 1

    2. Define Your Direction 13

    3. Develop Your Plan 27

    4. How To Create Instant And Sustainable Impact 43

    5. Elevate Your Leadership Skills 57

    6. Be A Team Player 69

    7. Expand Your Network 77

    8. Make Yourself Invaluable 89

    9. Build A Solid Foundation 107

   10. Avoid The Pitfalls 119

   11. Get Noticed 129

   12. Make Your Move 141

   13. Engage High-Potential Talent 153

   14. Senior Leader's Insights On Future Talent Needs 171

Appendix 191

About The Authors 219

ACKNOWLEDGEMENTS

We genuinely want to create a workplace where people feel encouraged and have a clear path to move forward in a way that promotes health, happiness, and heartfelt fulfillment.

Writing this book has been a journey filled with inspiration, learning, and growth. We are deeply thankful for the support, guidance, and encouragement from those who have walked alongside us every step of the way.

First and foremost, we extend our deepest gratitude to our husbands, Rob Powell and Greg Beyke. Your unwavering support, patience, and understanding have been the foundation of our efforts. Without your love and encouragement, this book would not have been possible.

A heartfelt thank you to our incredible book coach, Chrissy Das. Your insights, direction, and belief in our vision were instrumental in bringing this book to life. Your expertise has been invaluable, and we are immensely grateful for your partnership.

We also want to express our sincere appreciation to our Mastermind group—Victor Antonio, Ross Bernstein, Mark Hunter, Peter Stark, and Sam Richter. Your wisdom, feedback, and shared experiences have enriched our journey in ways words cannot adequately convey. You shape our thinking and inspire us to aim higher and work harder.

You Next

To everyone who has supported us along the way—whether through a kind word, a shared idea, participation in our focus groups, or a listening ear—thank you from the bottom of our hearts. This book reflects all the amazing people who have touched our lives and shaped our work.

With deepest gratitude,

Meridith Elliott Powell and Mary Kelly

INTRODUCTION

The frustration is real.

You feel like your career should be speeding down the highway, yet here you are—stuck behind a slow-moving cement truck on a one-lane road.

Many professionals experience this at some point. It's like your boss doesn't see or reward your efforts. Promotions keep slipping away to colleagues who seem less qualified. Senior executives hardly know you exist. All these unexpected roadblocks? Maddening.

We understand. As leadership experts, we've worked with thousands of people who know their careers should be advancing more quickly. Guiding these smart, talented professionals—often emerging or future leaders—to implement strategies that accelerate their success is one of our greatest passions.

So, what about you? Are you ready to fast-track your career? If so, you're in the right place. This book is the tool you need to shift your career into high gear. It's your life—get ready to take charge!

But first, let's address the elephant in the room: What's causing the career slowdown for so many bright, high-potential individuals?

Early in their careers, many people are highly motivated. They earn degrees and certifications, join key associations, volunteer, and network. Their goal? Land a great job at a thriving company—and they'll do whatever it takes to make that happen.

You Next

Once they get hired or promoted, it feels like they've reached the summit. All that hard work paid off! But then something happens: A new title or bigger paycheck lulls them into a passive career-planning mode. Let's be real. After years of pushing hard, who wouldn't want to ease off the gas pedal a bit? They might not even realize they're slowing down, but their comments reveal the truth:

"My boss seems happy with my work; I'm sure she mentions me to her manager."

"The company doesn't offer professional development, but I'm getting good experience."

"Maybe this is the year I'll get picked for a special assignment."

"No complaints from my team—so I must be doing okay!"

"Once someone recognizes my talent, I'll be considered for a promotion."

Here's the issue with this thinking: The career plan they so carefully crafted is fading into the background, leaving their success in other people's hands. It's like sliding into the passenger seat and letting someone else drive.

That's not how you climb the corporate ladder.

Instead of wondering what's next for your career, take back control and actively steer the course. By choosing the right path, you'll take charge of your future and redirect your career trajectory.

You Next Now will help you create a custom plan tailored to your career goals.

No matter what title you hold today, don't spend another day leaving your future to others. Take the driver's seat. We're confident you'll love the results, and we're excited to join you on this incredible journey!

CHAPTER ONE

WHERE Are You Now?

Are you ready to take charge of your career and accelerate your progress? Planning your career path can feel overwhelming, but the first step is gaining a clear understanding of where you are now. This chapter will guide you through that process, helping you assess your current position and set the stage for your next move.

CAREER SNAPSHOT: WHAT'S YOUR CURRENT STATUS?

It's time to get a clear understanding of where you stand. Read through the questions below and take a moment to really reflect on your answers. Write them down in the space provided in the worksheet in Appendix A, or download the fillable PDF version here: www.YouNextNow.com/Stateofthejobworksheet.

STATE OF THE JOB ASSESSMENT

- How long have you been with your current organization?
- How long have you been in your present role?
- What were your initial expectations when you transitioned into this position?
- How have your expectations evolved over time?
- Over the past 12 months, what aspects of your role have changed, and what has remained the same?
- What are the top three things you enjoy most about your job?
- What are the three most challenging aspects of your current job?
- Do you feel aligned with the organization but not your current role?
- Do you enjoy your role but feel the organization isn't the right fit?
- How well does your team collaborate and work together?
- Do you have a positive relationship with your current supervisor?
- If you could make a change in your role or responsibilities, what would it be?
- Are there realistic opportunities for advancement within your organization?

The purpose of answering these questions is to help you identify why you may be feeling stuck in your career. What's holding you back? If something is hindering your ability to build on your previous momentum, what's the roadblock?

Chapter One: Where Are You Now?

Is it your job?

Or (brace yourself) ... is it you?

No need to fear! Let's address those two questions.

HOW DO YOU KNOW IF YOU'RE STUCK IN A DEAD-END JOB?

Is your job the hold-up? It's not always easy to acknowledge that your career is stalled. Sometimes, the paycheck may blind you to the truth, or the benefits package may feel like a gilded cage. However, there are usually some telltale signs. See if any of these statements resonate with you.

You have zero motivation.

Your first thought in the morning is how much you dread going to work. You sit at your desk and wish you were anywhere else. Your energy level is low. You procrastinate, check social media, and find yourself watching funny dog videos for extended periods.

You feel unchallenged.

Everything about your job feels easy—and, frankly, boring. You've given all you have to your current position and sense that your talents would be better utilized elsewhere. You could do this job in your sleep, and sometimes that's exactly how it feels.

You haven't received a recent pay increase.

You're grateful for the monthly paycheck, but your boss hasn't offered any financial incentives to sweeten the deal. A good boss who truly appreciates you should always be considering ways to reward your efforts. It's been ages since you received a raise or bonus, and meanwhile, your expenses are rising while your Amazon wish list continues to grow.

You feel like an outsider on your team.

Even though you may have worked with your team members for years, you don't feel as though you fit in. Perhaps your ideas are routinely dismissed, or you're often conveniently left off the email about Happy Hour. Alternatively, you might feel like you're already carrying the team without the formal leadership title to match. Whatever the reason, there's a serious disconnect.

You don't feel heard.

You do your homework to come up with creative ideas and strong strategies, yet no matter how great they are, your boss ignores them. You start to wonder, why bother? This can go hand in hand with feeling unmotivated.

If any of these sound familiar, you may have identified the root of the problem: your job is draining the life out of you. For some, this realization provides the courage to quit outright or at least to begin an immediate search for new opportunities. For others, a tight job market or the necessity of paying the bills may require them to stay put. Either way, this book will provide you with a detailed game plan for moving forward.

But first, let's tackle a more pressing question:

Are you really
READY
to move up?

Is the hold-up you? When things aren't going our way, it's easy to focus on the external factors that impede our progress. We blame the economy, our boss, our team, and even the industry. We all do it at some point; it's part of being human. However, a strategic approach to career success requires a hefty dose of self-awareness. Internal reflection can be uncomfortable, but it's the foundation of this process.

Consider it this way: if a promotion became available tomorrow, would you truly be ready to step up? We're talking about your functional abilities, leadership skills, industry knowledge, communication style, and level of influence within the organization. All of it. The whole package. That's no small feat.

The good news is that these are all aspects you can control. If you realize you're not ready, you have the power to change that! The pages ahead will guide you through professional development upgrades to make you promotion-ready and poised for advancement.

But what happens in the meantime? You probably have some work to do, and you might also be feeling like you're going to lose your mind if you remain trapped in a less-than-optimal work environment.

That's why the rest of this chapter is dedicated to helping you maintain your sanity and sense of humor while you accelerate your career progress. Change will happen—but it probably won't happen overnight. If it does, please reach out and share your story! For everyone else, it's essential to have some survival skills to help you navigate the short-term career desert.

HOLDING PATTERN:
How can you manage in the meantime?

While you sharpen your skills and polish your resume, it's essential to maintain your day-to-day functionality and avoid feeling completely miserable. Life is short. Just knowing that you are actively implementing strategies to turbocharge your career should lift your spirits a bit. Beyond that, here are four actions you can take to help regain a sense of control over your professional future.

1. Have candid conversations with your supervisor.

You'd be surprised at the number of professionals who feel frustrated in their job situations yet never discuss these issues with their bosses. Bosses are not mind-readers; they need your help to supervise you effectively. They are human beings juggling multiple projects, various team members, and competing demands. Your career is likely not at the top of their priority list, so it's up to you to initiate the conversation.

Having a calm, strategic, and professional discussion with your supervisor about your current role and future opportunities can achieve several goals. Your boss will become aware of your interest and ambition. By openly expressing your thoughts on this matter, you'll feel less like a pressure cooker about to explode. Furthermore, initiating such discussions is an excellent way to demonstrate your leadership potential.

The truth is, most supervisors welcome a two-way dialogue about issues that impact team performance, as long as that dialogue is approached correctly. Tone, body language, and word choice are crucial. Consider starting the conversation with phrases like:

- "I'd like to talk about ways I can take on more responsibility."
- "I'd like to learn more about some of the more complex roles here."
- "I've been reflecting on my performance and would love your input on how I can contribute more effectively to our goals."
- "I'm interested in understanding our team's strategy better and where I might fit into our future plans."
- "Could we discuss potential opportunities for my professional growth within the team?"

- "I have some ideas that could improve our workflow and results. Can we set aside some time to discuss them?"
- "I'm eager to challenge myself and build on my current role; how can we make that happen together?"

> **Hint:** Avoid being argumentative, such as saying, "Here's a three-page list of my recent accomplishments that you have conveniently overlooked" or "Not that you've noticed, but I'm ready for a promotion."

We should pause for a moment to mention that a lack of job recognition can sometimes stem from insecure supervisors. Whether they acknowledge it or not, they might feel threatened by your skills, accomplishments, or visibility within the organization. Acknowledging your contributions might seem like it diminishes their own value. This can be particularly sensitive when you and your supervisor come from different generations, backgrounds, or social circles.

Be mindful of this potential tension and work deliberately to ease any fears. Ask for their advice and opinions, and express how much you appreciate their guidance. By building this relationship and fostering a greater level of trust and transparency, you'll pave the way for more productive conversations about your career.

2. Invest your time wisely.

Yes, you might find yourself temporarily stuck in a career holding pattern, which can feel terribly demotivating or even depressing. However, resist the temptation to let your mind fall into a similar pattern. Six months from now, you could look back and realize you drowned your professional sorrows in multiple gallons of Ben & Jerry's while binge-watching Game of Thrones twice. Alternatively, you could invest your time in learning new skills, taking online classes, and updating your LinkedIn profile. One of these options is far more likely to give you the career boost you truly desire.

Successful individuals tend to prioritize learning throughout their careers, with some even branching out into teaching after retirement. We recommend adopting this mindset now.

Investing your time wisely is about fueling your professional growth and expanding your capabilities. It's important to recognize that periods of career stagnation are not dead ends but opportunities to build a more robust set of skills and experiences. Here's how you can turn what feels like a standstill into a leap forward:

Conduct a self-audit to identify areas for improvement or entirely new skills that align with your future career aspirations. For example, if you're in marketing, consider learning about data analytics or digital advertising trends.

Utilize platforms such as Coursera or LinkedIn Learning, which offer courses taught by industry professionals. If you're in finance, aim to become proficient in new software, like advanced Excel techniques for financial modeling. Earning a certification such as the CFA or CPA can be a game changer.

Focus on soft skills that are increasingly in demand. Improving your communication skills can have a profound impact on your career trajectory at all levels. Graphic designers, for instance, can build a more robust portfolio, work on personal projects that showcase their skills, or even offer freelance services to expand their network and experience.

Leverage professional associations to connect with leaders in your field. Join webinars and virtual conferences, and participate in relevant discussions. By doing so, you're not just learning; you're also raising your profile and demonstrating initiative.

Document your growth by updating your LinkedIn page not only with new credentials but also with articles or posts that reflect your learning journey and thought leadership. This showcases your commitment to self-improvement and your willingness to engage with and contribute to your professional community.

Remember, the most successful people are lifelong learners. They don't wait for opportunities to come knocking; they build the door themselves.

Investing time in your professional development is never wasted. It's an investment that pays dividends in self-confidence, marketability, and ultimately career satisfaction. Whether through formal education, self-directed learning, or hands-on experience, every step you take to enhance your skills brings you closer to the future you envision for yourself.

3. Practice self-validation.

Don't let the lack of recognition from your supervisor or co-workers foster self-doubt. Reflect on your achievements and give yourself credit for a job well done. What qualifies as a big win for you this week? What have you learned? How will you apply that moving forward? Just because your boss neglects to provide positive feedback doesn't mean your hard work hasn't made a difference. That's something to celebrate, even if it's a party of one.

Here's the caveat: Before you break out the pompoms to cheer for your unprecedented success, ensure that you're being realistic. Can you quantify the value you've added? Are your efforts genuinely extraordinary, or are they more in the realm of "slightly exceeding expectations"? How does your work truly compare with that of your peers? Strive to maintain a healthy sense of objectivity when determining whether your performance deserves a standing ovation, some nice applause, or simply the satisfaction of another paycheck.

Should you take pride in your work? Yes!

Should you inflate your sense of worth? No!

In a team meeting, the distinction between taking pride in your work and inflating your worth can manifest in both your behavior and communication.

When you take pride in your work, you:

1. Share achievements with humility and grace. You might say, "I'm pleased with how our project turned out, and I'm grateful for the team's support. Here's what we accomplished..."

2. Acknowledge the team's effort. Even if it was your initiative, you recognize the collaborative effort: "While I initially led the X initiative, it was the hard work of the entire team that brought us this success."

3. Focus on results that benefit everyone. Your conversation is results-oriented rather than self-centered: "The strategy we implemented increased productivity by X%, and I'm excited to see how we can build on this."

Conversely, inflating your worth means you:

1. Dominate the conversation. You might continually steer discussions back to your contributions, overshadowing the efforts of others.

2. Take undue credit. Statements like "Without my input, project X wouldn't have succeeded" suggest that the success hinged solely on you.

3. Overemphasize your role. Using "I" instead of "we," as in "I made this project a success," implies it was a solo effort rather than a team endeavor.

In a healthy team environment, confidence and pride should be balanced with humility and gratitude. By appreciating the collaborative nature of success, you foster a more inclusive and supportive team dynamic.

4. Remain ready to move up or move on.

As you begin implementing strategies to advance your career, there's one significant unknown you must acknowledge: the time horizon for advancement. You might enroll in a semester-long development course and soon discover an incredible job lead by networking with fellow students. Your new attitude and behavior could catch your boss's attention at just the right moment for a promotion or special assignment. You never know...

That's why the scout motto applies here: "Be prepared!" Keep your resume updated with your latest courses and skills. Ensure your LinkedIn profile is current and presents you in the most positive light. If you view your search for a new position—whether internal or external—as an ongoing journey, you'll always be ready to leap ahead when the right opportunity arises.

Now that you have a clear understanding of your current situation and know how to manage it while taking steps to move forward, you're ready to accelerate your career progress.

Next stop? Developing your personal career advancement strategy.

MAKE IT HAPPEN!

➢ Be honest about your current career status.

➢ Complete the "State of the Job" assessment for greater insight at YouNextNow.com/StateoftheJobWorksheet.

➢ Evaluate whether you are in a dead-end job.

➢ Analyze your true readiness for advancement.

➢ Manage holding-pattern frustrations with targeted actions.

For more valuable tips, visit YouNextNow.com!

CHAPTER TWO

DEFINE
Your Direction

Clark had been working for a commercial real estate company for nine years. He joined the firm right after graduating with a business degree, and he was the first to admit that it wasn't a great fit and not his ideal job. However, at the time, the job market was slow, and he and his wife had just celebrated the birth of their first child.

He always intended to search for something else, but life got busy, and it never seemed to be the right time. Two more children came along, and Clark's wife decided to quit her job to stay home with the kids. With his growing responsibilities, advancing his career—whether with his current employer or elsewhere—was simply not his top priority.

Though he was well-liked and respected among his colleagues, he didn't feel qualified to move up or have the bandwidth to launch a full-fledged job search.

Clark needed the paycheck, and he felt stuck.

HAVE YOU EVER FELT STUCK IN YOUR CAREER?

Even the most well-intentioned professionals can find their careers stuck on autopilot. One workday blurs into the next, then into a week, a month, and before you know it, years have passed—and your career is simply coasting along. You may feel unfulfilled or even unhappy. While shifting gears and heading in a new direction can be challenging, it's absolutely possible!

The fact that you're reading this book shows that you're ready to hit reset and take control of your journey. Congratulations!

In this chapter, we'll guide you step-by-step through the process of defining your career direction and leveraging your greatest strengths. We'll delve into your career assets, values, purpose, and personal vision to help you craft a powerful career advancement strategy.

 YOUR CAREER ASSETS:

What do you do?

At first glance, that might seem like a simple question. "I'm an accountant." "I'm in sales." "I work in HR."

But not so fast.

We want to dig deeper and examine this topic through four key lenses: your talents, skills, education, and experience. We'll define each category and provide examples to clarify the distinction.

Talents: Your natural and innate aptitudes.

Imagine being born with the gift of perfect pitch and the uncanny ability to replicate any melody after hearing it just once.

"By age two, little Sydney was already a musical prodigy!"

Chapter Two: Define Your Direction

Skills: Proficiency is what you gain by honing your natural abilities through consistent effort.

To truly develop raw talent, you must invest time and practice regularly.

"Hey Sydney, how do you get to Carnegie Hall? Practice, practice, practice!"

Education: Knowledge you deliberately acquire in a specific field.

To maximize your skills, you must study the technical aspects—music theory, composition, and production.

"Sydney's been accepted to Juilliard on a full scholarship!"

Experience: Consistent practice of applying a skill to refine and master it.

To grow, you must integrate your talent, skill, and education through regular performances, gaining invaluable insights that only come from real-world application.

"Sydney played at countless parties, coffee shops, and local restaurants before landing her big break with a record label."

> **The Takeaway:** Your career success hinges on how effectively you integrate these four components to present yourself as a valuable, marketable asset to both current and future employers.

Talent alone won't get you far without the hard work to build on it through learning and practice. On the flip side, hard work can't compensate for a lack of natural aptitude. You might practice basketball 14 hours a day and study every detail of the game, but at 5'2", your odds of making it to the NBA are slim. And when it comes to experience? While your doctor may seem well-educated, would you be eager to volunteer as the patient for her first-ever brain surgery? Yeah, didn't think so.

Think of these four components—talent, skills, education, and experience—as your unique set of career assets, which you're packaging and "selling" to potential employers. In this case, you are the product. Instead of attracting customers to buy your product, rave about it online, and remain loyal, you're aiming to get noticed, hired, promoted, and recognized. The concept is the same.

So, what does your "product" look like to an employer? Use the space below to identify your personal career assets.

YOUR CAREER ASSETS

Talents: What are your natural gifts?

Skills: What abilities have you developed and refined to enhance your career and advance your expertise?

Education: What learning opportunities have you pursued?

Experience: How much time have you dedicated to applying your career assets in practical, real-world scenarios?

See Appendix B for Your Career Assets Worksheet.

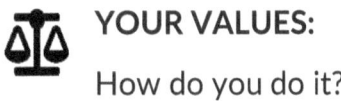 YOUR VALUES:
How do you do it?

Now, we're transitioning from what you do to how you do it.

This step invites you to examine your personal values more closely. These values reflect who you are and what you believe. They're often shaped by your upbringing, the lessons you've learned, and how you aspire to live. If you're eager to accelerate your career, it's essential to understand the values that motivate you.

One effective way to clarify your values is to consider this process from a corporate perspective. Businesses frequently engage in similar exercises. Here are a few well-known examples:

- ✓ *Southwest Airlines*

    Values: Friendly, Respectful, Passionate, Customer-Focused, Fun

- ✓ *Airbnb*

    Values: Caring, Adventurous, Hospitable, Resourceful, Flexible

- ✓ *Apple*

    Values: Innovative, Collaborative, Enthusiastic, Ambitious, Bold

> **Take Note:** Not a single mention of transportation, lodging, or computers! It's all about the "flavor" these brands want to project to the world and their customers.

When leaders at these companies decide which strategic paths to follow, they consider whether those choices align with the values they've established. Their values serve as a solid guidepost for decision-making. Does this move "feel" like us, or would it seem completely out of character? This explains why Southwest Airlines likely won't start hiring a group of grumpy individuals with no customer service experience, and Apple won't issue a press release announcing they're out of new ideas for technology improvements.

The same principle applies to you and your career. When you clearly define your personal values, you establish a specific standard for making everyday decisions and keeping your career on track. Your personal values can help you seek out companies that share similar values. Once defined, use your values as a litmus test: if a career aligns with your values, then it is the right career for you; if not, keep searching!

Let's break this down. As you perform your job, which values guide your choices and decisions? What attributes and characteristics define who you are as a person and a professional? Filling in these blanks might give you a head start.

My family and friends say they appreciate that I am

_____

My co-workers say they can always count on me to be

_____

I'm proud that I am

_____

Chapter Two: Define Your Direction

Now, take a moment to review the list below and circle all the values that resonate with you. Feel free to add any additional values that you identify:

- Accepting
- Adaptable
- Appreciative
- Attentive
- Careful
- Collaborative
- Committed
- Compassionate
- Concerned
- Considerate
- Consistent
- Cooperative
- Creative
- Decisive
- Dependable
- Determined
- Diligent
- Discerning
- Effective
- Efficient
- Enthusiastic

- Flexible
- Friendly
- Generous
- Grateful
- Hard-Working
- Honest
- Humble
- Joyful
- Kind
- Loving
- Loyal
- Optimistic
- Patient
- Flexible
- Persistent
- Persuasive
- Purposeful
- Reliable
- Resilient
- Resourceful
- Respectful

- Fair
- Fearless
- Flexible
- Friendly
- Generous
- Grateful
- Hard-Working
- Honest
- Fearless
- Responsible
- Sincere
- Tactful
- Team-Oriented
- Trustworthy
- Truthful
- Understanding
- Other_____
- Other_____

If you've circled several value words, consider narrowing down the list to your top 3 to 5 choices for clarity.

YOUR CORE VALUES

_____ _____ _____ _____ _____

See Appendix C to complete the Your Values Exercise.

As you move forward, ensure that you clearly project your positive values in all your actions. **When your behaviors and attitudes align with these values, you will solidify your image as a candidate ready for immediate career advancement.**

 YOUR PURPOSE:
Why do you do it?

Consider the reasons behind everything you do. What motivates you to pursue a career in your industry? What kind of impact are you making? What is your "why"?

Unless you're independently wealthy, the obvious answer to the question "Why do you work?" is to pay your bills. While that's true, it isn't the focus of this discussion. Dig deeper. Here are some examples:

"I'm a doctor because I want to care for my patients so they can live happy, healthy lives."

"I'm a teacher because I want to have a lasting impact on young children who will become the future leaders of our world."

Chapter Two: Define Your Direction

"I'm a banker because I love helping my customers manage their money effectively so they can achieve their financial goals and pursue their dreams worry-free."

Now it's your turn. What's your career purpose? Why do you do what you do? Who are you serving? Why does it matter?

YOUR PURPOSE STATEMENT

That's a tough question, isn't it? To be fair, writing a purpose statement can be a real struggle for some people. However, if you find yourself in that category, you may have uncovered a contributing factor to your career slowdown. It's impossible to be passionate—and ultimately successful—doing something that feels aimless or unfocused from your perspective.

Without absolute clarity on your "WHY," you'll never be fully committed to your "WHAT." That can land an otherwise promising career in a giant pothole along the side of the road.

Continue to refine your thought process to more clearly define your purpose. What are you on this earth to achieve? Are you motivated to change the lives of others, transform an industry, or create something truly innovative?

Once you can concisely articulate your purpose, you can begin to tackle the bigger questions:

1. Is your current position setting you up to fulfill that purpose?
2. If not, what type of job would?
3. What role would make you leap out of bed in the morning, filled with energy and eager to tackle the day's challenges?
4. What type of organization would you be working for?
5. What does a purpose-driven, you-focused career path look like?

You may not have perfect clarity on all of this right now, but it's excellent food for thought as you move forward!

You Next

Go ahead and draft your purpose statement.

Your Purpose Statement

```
┌─────────────────────────────────────┐
│                                     │
│                                     │
│                                     │
└─────────────────────────────────────┘
```

What resonates with you, and where do you need to reflect further? Make a note to revisit this later if you need more clarity.

 YOUR VISION:

What's your end game?

So far, you've conducted a thorough inventory of your current career status. However, before you can chart a course forward, you need to identify your ultimate destination. Where do you envision yourself ending up? What would you like to achieve by the end of your career that will enable you to fulfill your purpose? Defining a vision that encompasses both your life and career is essential.

Hello, Meridith here! When I first crafted my career vision, I focused solely on my professional aspirations: the job I desired, the skills I needed, and the impact I wanted to make. I was fully committed and pushing hard to reach my goals. Unfortunately, this relentless pursuit led me to a town I didn't want to live in, a strained marriage due to my excessive work hours, and a role in a company and industry I wasn't truly passionate about. I had achieved my career vision, but I had overlooked my life.

We challenge you to create a personal vision statement that clearly addresses both your career and life aspirations in an easy-to-remember format.

Chapter Two: Define Your Direction

To begin, you'll need to define your career assets, values, and purpose. When these elements are robust and focused, they will create a direct line to your vision, or at the very least, provide you with a strong foundation. Additionally, consider including your goals for work-life balance and your desire to engage with the community.

- ✓ **Career Assets**
- ✓ **Values**
- ✓ **Purpose**
- ✓ **Personal Vision Statement**

Here's an example:

- o **Career Assets:** A talented architect with impressive credentials and ten years of experience.
- o **Values:** Determined, team-oriented, friendly, creative, and enthusiastic.
- o **Purpose:** To design buildings that transform and enhance how people utilize their corporate office spaces.
- o **Personal Vision Statement:** I aspire to become the CEO of a successful architecture firm where employees are excited to come to work and collaborate on developing unique, award-winning commercial buildings.

It's clear how these components connect and flow naturally. Ready to give it a try? Dream big. No barriers, no limitations—just imagine endless possibilities. The sky's the limit! Start by jotting down some initial thoughts for your personal career vision statement.

YOUR VISION STATEMENT

Is your direction clear? If you're struggling to see a straightforward path connecting the elements of your vision statement, don't worry—this book will guide you. In the meantime, ask yourself if limiting beliefs might be holding you back. We all have those nagging inner messages that can cloud our vision. Do any of these sound familiar?

"I'm terrible at math, so I'll never succeed in a numbers-driven role."

"I could never be a good salesperson because I'm an introvert."

"I'm just not creative."

"I avoid team projects because I work better alone."

We could write an entire book on overcoming limiting beliefs like these, but here's the bottom line: Don't let those messages stand between you and your goals. Maybe math isn't your strong suit. So what? If you're a great leader, you can hire someone to handle the numbers. There are always solutions to help you reach your dreams, even if it means partnering with others along the way. Don't create barriers for yourself!

You might already be rethinking parts of your vision statement, and that's okay—revisions are natural! In fact, you'll likely update and refine your vision multiple times throughout this book. (You should also plan to revisit your vision statement annually to ensure it still aligns with your goals.) Now that you've outlined your direction and have a sense of where you want to go, let's start mapping out how to get there.

Your Vision Statement

MAKE IT HAPPEN!

- ➤ Establish the ideal direction for your career.
- ➤ Identify the unique career assets that define your expertise: talents, skills, education, and experience.
- ➤ Highlight the core values that guide how you perform your work.
- ➤ Clearly articulate your professional purpose.
- ➤ Define and clarify your long-term career vision.

For more valuable tips, visit YouNextNow.com!

CHAPTER THREE

DEVELOP
Your Plan

Bridget had been with her law firm for eight years. Intelligent and driven, she was one of the youngest ever promoted to a management role. But what Bridget truly wanted was to become a partner. Based on her track record, that seemed like the natural next step—just not to those making the decisions.

Understandably, Bridget was frustrated. No matter how hard she worked or how many hours she put in, it didn't seem to make a difference. As time dragged on, self-doubt crept in, and resentment began to build.

Totally understandable, right? But what Bridget really needed was to leverage her sharp legal mind to build a solid case for her advancement. Instead of passively hoping for a promotion, she could take a proactive, strategic approach.

We often tell our clients: hope is not a strategy. If you want to take control of your career, you need to plan for success and make it happen—one step at a time. That's exactly what we're focusing on in this chapter.

So far, you've assessed your skills and values (where you are today) and defined your vision (where you want to go). Now, it's time to map out a deliberate path from Point A to Point B.

Let's get tactical. This is the practical, roll-up-your-sleeves-and-get-it-done part of the process. If that sounds a little intimidating, don't worry. We're going to make it simple and straightforward.

CAREER DEVELOPMENT: HOW DO YOU GET THERE?

The first step in building a solid plan for your career development is identifying the key attributes needed to achieve your career vision. In other words, you need to create a clear, detailed picture of what your ultimate success looks like.

But let's take it a step further. Envision your success so vividly that you can see it, feel it, hear it, taste it—and sure, why not—even smell it. Engage every sense in visualizing your goal until it feels real, tangible, and within reach.

Can you see it in your mind now?

No matter what your vision is, start by listing the qualifications and attributes someone in that role would need. For example, if your goal is to become a top-tier CEO, your list might include the following credentials and traits:

SAMPLE VISION PROFILE: CEO

- Advanced degree (MBA or PhD)
- Multiple continuing education credits
- Relevant industry certifications
- Broad knowledge across various subjects (well-read)
- Exceptional business, management, and operational skills

- Expertise as a strategic, results-oriented thinker
- Strong communication, listening, and public speaking abilities
- Proven relationship-building and collaborative work skills
- High emotional intelligence (self-awareness, social awareness, resilience, flexibility, humility, empathy, poise, presence, etc.)
- Refined ability to inspire and influence others
- Recognized industry leader
- Active community involvement and name recognition
- Extensive business-world connections
- Experience as a successful coach and mentor
- Reputation for honesty, ambition, decisiveness, generosity, and enthusiasm

If that list seems overwhelming, take a deep breath. You don't need to possess every single quality and characteristic to achieve your vision. People often take different paths but end up in the same place. Think of these vision qualities as an optimal goal, but don't worry about matching them exactly. You know the saying about aiming for the moon but still being thrilled to land among the stars? That's the idea here.

Flexibility is key. Maybe pursuing an advanced degree doesn't fit your current lifestyle or budget. No worries—there are plenty of free or affordable ways to expand your knowledge if you know where to look!

You might also notice something missing from the list: a statement like "25 years of experience." There's a reason for that. People progress at different rates, and there's no magic number of years—whether 10 or 20—that suddenly makes you ready for advancement.

While experience does matter (remember the brain surgeon analogy?), think of it more in terms of "experiences." What variety of experiences, both inside and outside of your organization, will

You Next

equip you to tackle the challenges of your vision-based role? It's not just about time served; it's about the value of the experiences you've gained.

Now, ready to give this a shot? Re-read your personal vision statement from Chapter Two and pull out all the necessary qualities for that role—considering education, hard and soft skills, experiences, values, and attributes. Add as much detail as possible. Paint a vivid picture with your words!

Chapter Three: Develop Your Plan

YOUR VISION PROFILE:

Position/Title: _____

- _____
- _____
- _____
- _____
- _____
- _____
- _____

What you've accomplished in that exercise is the beginning of framing your mission in terms of career development goals. Great job!

In Chapter Two, you pinpointed your starting point by identifying your natural talents, skills, education, experience, and values. Your ideal destination can be found in the list above. Now you've got Point A and Point B clearly defined. What does this mean for you? If your career isn't moving at the pace you'd like, you now have the precise GPS coordinates to help guide you along the most direct path.

To make this information easier to digest, it's helpful to combine your Point A and Point B into a single chart, organized by categories. Let's revisit the CEO example, comparing the current status of our fictitious professional with the qualities needed to achieve that career vision:

SAMPLE GAP MAP

	TODAY: Junior Manager	VISION: CEO
Talents/ Skills	Finance, Operations	Business, Operations, Communications
Emotional Intelligence	Average	Very High
Education:	Bachelor's Degree in Finance	MBA, Continuing Education, Industry Certifications
Experience(s)	Bank Teller, Junior Manager	Multiple Organizations/Departments/Roles, Progressive Leadership Responsibilities; Successful Coach/Mentor; Past President of Industry Association; Board of Directors for a Local Nonprofit; Community Involvement; Well-Connected.
Values/ Reputation	Hard-Working, Dependable, Kind	Driven, Decisive, Enthusiastic

Now it's your turn! To gain clarity and specificity about your career development needs, let's consolidate your current status and vision into a single chart. On the left-hand side, transfer the information you gathered from Chapter Two. On the right-hand side, categorize and list the qualities you've identified for your career vision.

Chapter Three: Develop Your Plan

YOUR GAP MAP

	TODAY:	VISION:
Talents/Skills		
Emotional Intelligence		
Education:		
Experience(s)		
Values/Reputation		

Right there, in those two columns, you can now clearly see the exact gaps that need to be filled to achieve your career vision. Mic drop! Cue the enthusiastic cheers of a roaring crowd. We're giving you a virtual high-five right now!

Now, using your Gap Map, start brainstorming ways to close the gap in each category and move closer to your career vision. The possibilities are endless, but here are a few ideas to get you started:

Apply for a leadership training program	Learn from a coach/mentor
Ask for increased responsibilities	Participate in a rotation group
Attend conferences/workshops	Present a paper at a seminar

33

Be more deliberate with networking	Pursue continuing education credits
Consider changing employers	Read targeted books/articles/blogs
Develop targeted skills	Request an overseas assignment
Earn industry certifications	Serve as an officer of a club/group
Enroll in graduate school	Shadow a colleague
Explore lateral moves	Sign up for an online course/webinar
Find outside leadership opportunities	Take on a research project
Follow industry/business influencers	Volunteer to lead a special initiative
Get involved in community service	Work with an accountability partner
Join an industry association/committee	

Take a moment to write down the top contenders in each category below. What actions can you take to cultivate the qualities and characteristics of someone who has realized your career vision? At this stage, don't impose any limitations on your list. Imagine you have the financial means, resources, and time to pursue all possibilities. We'll refine the list later!

YOUR TARGETED GAP FILLERS

	TODAY:	VISION:
Talents/ Skills		
Emotional Intelligence		
Education:		
Experience(s)		
Values/ Reputation		

See Appendix D for the Gap Map resources.

VISION QUEST: WHERE DO YOU START?

Next up, you will identify how to start addressing that list of gap fillers needed to propel you toward your vision more swiftly.

Some individuals work in Fortune 500 companies that offer extensive career development opportunities, while others are employed at small startups where the CEO leads the company, brews the coffee, and occasionally replenishes the printer paper. Regardless of the situation (and everything in between), one truth remains: YOU are responsible for taking charge of your professional development. No one else is more invested in your career success than you are. Period.

Now is the perfect time to dust off your proactive attitude and prepare it for full-time duty.

Remember that no-limits brainstorming from the previous section? It's time for a reality check. Take stock of the development resources currently available to you through your employer or other connections. These may include tuition reimbursement, access to online courses, rotation groups, leadership programs, coaching or mentoring options, or a knowledge portal.

Current Development Resources Available

_____

_____

_____

Now, let's expand on that! Where can you go or what actions can you take to access additional development tools and experiences? If that sounds costly, you'll be pleased to know that affordable alternatives, scholarships, special considerations, and hidden opportunities are always available for those who are determined enough to seek them out!

Additional Development Options

_____

_____

_____

Chapter Three: Develop Your Plan

✅ ACTION PLAN:
How do you make it happen?

Now it's time to transform those clearly defined gap fillers into robust action plans. Here's the key point to remember: This is a long-term endeavor. There's no magic pill that will propel you from Junior Manager to CEO in just thirty minutes. (Wouldn't that be wonderful?) Achieving your goals takes time—and a commitment to a marathon-not-a-sprint mindset. However, if you dedicate yourself to making small improvements each day, you may be surprised at how swiftly you can advance toward your ultimate objective.

Begin by breaking down your gap-filler activities into manageable steps, and consider how you can realistically integrate them into your life over time (without compromising your well-being!). Use the space below to outline your action plan as a deliberate, cumulative effort that will purposefully and consistently enhance your career value over time.

ACTION PLAN
Things You Can Do Starting Today

	TODAY:	VISION:
Talents/ Skills		
Emotional Intelligence		
Education:		
Experience(s)		

You Next

Values/Reputation		

Things You Can Do Within the Next 12 Months

	TODAY:	VISION:
Talents/Skills		
Emotional Intelligence		
Education:		
Experience(s)		
Values/Reputation		

Things You can Do Within the Next Five Years

	TODAY:	VISION:
Talents/Skills		
Emotional Intelligence		
Education:		
Experience(s)		

Chapter Three: Develop Your Plan

Values/ Reputation		

See Appendix E for a blank copy of the Action Plan.

While this activity is still fresh in your mind, capitalize on the momentum you've built. What changes can you initiate right now? Which helpful books can you download to your Kindle? Are there online courses that align perfectly with the gap fillers you've identified? Can you share your goals with a friend or colleague who can support and motivate you along the way? The most crucial aspect of an action plan is the ACTION. No one else can take those steps for you.

You have your map in hand. Let the journey begin!

BAD HABITS: HOW DO YOU LET GO?

Before we conclude this chapter, let's address an issue many professionals encounter as they embark on a career-boosting initiative. You may be eager to move forward, diligently following your map and adhering to your timeline, but first, ask yourself a critical question:

Did your past career frustrations subtly introduce unproductive work habits that need to be identified and eliminated?

This can happen to the best of us! Be honest. Do any of these resonate with you?

Getting distracted easily	Not prioritizing your health
Neglecting time management	Being late frequently

Being overcommitted	Wasting time
Not having clarity about goals/priorities	Refusing to delegate
Refusing to accept help/feedback	Having a negative attitude
Being disorganized	Complaining about tasks/people
Procrastinating	Allowing "digital device overload"
Communicating ineffectively	Multitasking in an inefficient way
Being inflexible	Feeling like a victim

Sometimes, these bad habits can creep in and become standard operating procedure before we even realize there's been an invasion. As you begin implementing new strategies to accelerate your career, ensure you STOP the behaviors that could undermine your efforts. It's a new chapter, a clean slate—it's time to eliminate all bad habits!

MAKE IT HAPPEN!

- Develop a strategic plan to achieve your career vision.
- Identify the career assets necessary to reach your goals.
- Assess your current career assets against those required for your vision.
- Pinpoint targeted opportunities for professional development.
- Create an actionable plan with a functional timeline.
- Eliminate any habits that may be hindering your progress.

For more valuable tips, visit YouNextNow.com!

CHAPTER FOUR

HOW TO
Create Instant and Sustainable Impact

Antonio was enthusiastic and ambitious—a true go-getter. One thing he wasn't? Patient. This isn't surprising; he grew up in an era of instant news, on-demand entertainment, and 24/7 support teams. However, living in a world filled with immediate results can lead to an expectation of instant gratification in everything we do.

When Antonio was selected for a leadership training program at his telecommunications company, he and his peers were asked to create career development plans spanning the next five years. To Antonio, that timeframe might as well have been 500 years. Sixty months felt like an eternity, fraught with unpredictable variables and at least five new iPhone models on the horizon. Can we really plan for that?

Despite his skepticism, Antonio mapped out his potential career path and identified the development needs he needed to address along the way. One week later, he was already applying his characteristic sense of urgency to the entire process. He had signed up for two online workshops, investigated local MBA programs designed for full-time professionals, purchased four new books to read, and was actively "interviewing" mentors.

Kudos to Antonio for his proactive approach! Unfortunately, it's not possible to cram five years of development into three months. It takes time. Antonio, however, was not a fan of waiting. He believed that if he put in significant effort, he was ready for that increased paycheck and the accompanying job.

We've worked with many professionals in the same position. They have the satisfaction of knowing they're putting all the pieces in place to reach their goals, but the waiting drives them crazy. They want results NOW. Fifteen minutes ago.

While we can't speed up time, we can help people like Antonio take steps to gain faster career traction while working toward their larger development goals. That's the focus of this chapter.

You don't have to feel stuck in a holding pattern while pursuing your long-term plans. You can start right now to elevate your perceived career potential by upgrading six specific areas to produce more immediate **IMPACT**:

Chapter Four: How To Create Instant and Sustainable Impact

Show INITIATIVE
Increase Your MARKETABILITY
Exude PROFESSIONALISM
Maintain a Positive ATTITUDE
Build Your CREDIBILITY
Be THANKFUL

Yes, we really love a great acronym. It helps us remember stuff. Don't judge.

1. Show INITIATIVE

Demonstrate to your supervisor that you are self-motivated and passionate about your work. This means taking initiative without waiting for direction or guidance. Set your own goals and deadlines for open-ended projects, and make thoughtful suggestions for process improvements or ways to enhance customer service. If every aspect of your current job bores you, brainstorm ways to make it more engaging. Your boss will undoubtedly be impressed if you arrive with relevant ideas that could boost engagement for both you and your team.

Increase your participation in meetings and share your opinions. Just ensure you've done your homework in advance and have something substantial to contribute. Speaking just for the sake of saying something is not effective participation; there are plenty of people who attend meetings just to hear themselves talk.

If you know the topics to be discussed in an upcoming meeting, conduct an online search for related articles or blogs about industry trends, competitive moves, or technological advances.

Find something worthwhile to share. When you do speak up, remember that your goal is to add value to the discussion—not merely to provide interesting trivia.

Reinforce your willingness to continue learning. Successful leaders view education as a never-ending process; they actively seek out new skills to master and mindsets worth adopting. Mirroring this attitude, it is essential to commit to a journey of perpetual learning and growth. Recognizing that there is always room for improvement and knowledge acquisition is crucial for demonstrating your potential as a leader. Instead of focusing on proving how much you know, embrace the opportunity to expand your horizons, challenge perspectives, and evolve both personally and professionally. Acknowledge that there's always room for growth rather than continually trying to prove your knowledge.

Volunteer for challenging projects, especially those that offer a chance to take on a leadership role. By stepping up when others hesitate, you not only demonstrate your initiative and dedication but also showcase your ability to handle difficult situations with confidence and competence. Taking on such projects allows you to develop and refine your leadership skills, making you a more valuable asset to the team.

Moreover, your manager will certainly remember your willingness to tackle tough assignments during your next review, potentially opening doors to new opportunities, promotions, and greater responsibilities. Embracing these challenges can significantly contribute to your personal and professional growth, positioning you as a proactive and reliable leader within the organization.

Identify a skill or tool that could help you perform your job more efficiently.

Identify a skill or tool that can enhance your job performance and efficiency. Begin by thoroughly assessing your current workflow to pinpoint areas where improvements can be made. Conduct research to determine which specific skill or tool would best address these needs. This might involve reading industry reports, consulting colleagues, or exploring online resources and reviews.

Once you have identified a promising solution, investigate what it would entail to acquire this new skill or tool. This may include understanding the costs of purchasing new equipment, the time and resources required for training, and any potential impacts on your current workload.

After gathering the necessary information, prepare a proposal for your boss. Outline the benefits of the new skill or tool, including how it will enhance productivity, improve work quality, and potentially reduce costs or increase revenue. Highlight relevant case studies or success stories from other companies or teams that have implemented similar improvements. Be sure to include a clear plan for how you will learn the new skill or utilize the new tool, specifying the timeline, required resources, and any support you might need from your manager or team.

By presenting a well-researched and thoughtfully constructed proposal, you demonstrate your commitment to continuous improvement and your proactive approach to problem-solving. This shows that you are serious about working smarter and positions you as a forward-thinking and resourceful team member likely to contribute to the organization's success. Your boss will be highly impressed!

Exhibit your sense of perseverance by powering your way through large projects. Persist in the face of tough obstacles by breaking overwhelming tasks into manageable chunks. Demonstrate your ability to embrace challenges and devise effective solutions to complex problems.

2. Increase your MARKETABILITY

Position yourself as the highly engaged team member who deserves a promotion. Find ways to demonstrate that you genuinely care about achieving the organization's mission and vision. When a supervisor sees your willingness to prioritize the company's interests over your own, it signals that you can handle the responsibilities that come with a more prominent title.

One of our coaching clients noticed an inefficiency in her department. We worked with Janet, who is in the marketing department of a mid-sized tech company. She observed that the process of launching new marketing campaigns often faced delays due to a lack of coordination between the marketing, sales, and IT departments. Recognizing this as an opportunity to enhance her value and marketability, she decided to take action.

Janet conducted a thorough analysis of the current process and identified significant bottlenecks. She researched best practices for cross-functional collaboration and proposed a streamlined process. With our guidance, Janet presented her findings and suggestions to her manager, emphasizing how these changes could lead to faster campaign launches, better alignment between departments, and ultimately, increased revenue.

With her manager's approval, Janet volunteered to lead a cross-functional project team to implement the new process. She scheduled regular meetings with representatives from marketing, sales, and IT, ensuring everyone was aligned and communicated effectively. Janet collaborated with her manager to set clear goals and timelines, monitor progress, and routinely adjust the plan as needed to overcome obstacles.

Throughout the project, Janet demonstrated her dedication to the company's mission and vision. She worked extra hours when necessary, offered support to team members, and remained focused on the project's success. Janet also provided regular updates to her manager and other stakeholders on the project's progress, showcasing her leadership skills and commitment to achieving the organization's goals.

Janet's proactive approach, leadership, and dedication were noticed. Her manager recognized her contributions and recommended her for a promotion during the next review cycle. Janet's increased marketability positioned her as a key asset to the company, opening new opportunities for career advancement.

3. Exude PROFESSIONALISM

Consistently look, sound, and act like someone who is ready to ascend the corporate ladder. What does professionalism look like in today's corporate world?

Professionalism encompasses being a cooperative and supportive team member, treating everyone with respect, sharing knowledge, offering help, and valuing diverse perspectives. Effective professionals understand that collective efforts lead to better outcomes and are willing to prioritize team goals over personal ambitions.

Professionalism applies to every aspect of your presence: verbal, nonverbal, and visual. What unspoken message are you sending about your capacity to perform in an elevated role? Are you an impeccable professional or a wrinkled couch potato?

We're not just talking about upgrading your wardrobe, although that is certainly an important component. Beyond dressing neatly and appropriately, be strategic about your word choices and sentence structure. Are your comments in team meetings well-organized and coherent, or are they littered with "umms" and "likes" to the point of distraction? Is your tone of voice and body language more aligned with that of a CEO or an incoming college freshman? Be deliberate about ensuring the whole package of YOU appears ready for prime-time advancement.

One of our favorite CEOs absolutely detested hearing the word "like" as a filler. In his meetings, he would stop anyone who used the word "like" and say, "Start over." Sometimes it took the employee ten attempts to express three sentences without using the word "like." While this might seem harsh, he was training his team to be more articulate and sound more confident when they spoke. Because he applied this standard to everyone, he was perceived as fair and earned their respect.

4. **Maintain a Positive ATTITUDE**

Inspire those around you with an infectiously positive attitude. Here's why attitude matters: given a choice, everyone would prefer to work with—and promote—people who maintain a positive outlook. In fact, leaders often hire candidates who may be less skilled if their attitudes serve as morale boosters for the entire team. Job skills can be taught, but a negative attitude is much harder to change.

With this in mind, strive to show up every day with the intention of positively influencing and inspiring those around you, regardless of your position. One aspect you can control is the attitude you project each day. Aim to keep your outlook consistently positive. While you may not love every moment of your job, you can approach it with a glass-half-full mindset. At the very least, smile as you remind yourself that this role is a valuable stepping stone toward your next level—whether that's in your current company or elsewhere.

We understand that being cheerful and positive every day is not always easy, especially when complaining seems to be a national pastime. Did you know there's actual science behind why people love to complain? Complaining is a common human behavior, and it involves a fascinating blend of psychological and neurobiological factors.

Neurochemical Rewards

When people complain, their brains often release dopamine—a neurotransmitter linked to pleasure and reward. This release produces a temporary sense of satisfaction or relief, akin to the feelings one experiences from other rewarding activities, such as indulging in comfort food or receiving social approval.

Cognitive Biases

Human brains are hardwired to notice and remember negative experiences more vividly than positive ones—a phenomenon known as negativity bias. This bias likely evolved as a survival mechanism, enabling our ancestors to recognize and avoid dangers. Consequently, people tend to focus on and discuss negative experiences more often.

Social Bonding

Complaining can act as a social bonding tool. Sharing grievances with others fosters a sense of solidarity and mutual understanding, strengthening social connections and cultivating a feeling of belonging.

Attention and Validation

Complaining can draw attention and validation from others. When someone voices their grievances, they often receive empathy and support from listeners, which can be both reassuring and affirming. This external validation reinforces the behavior and is particularly prevalent on social media. For instance, if you share good news, you might receive a handful of responses. However, if you post about finding a bug in your salad at a restaurant, the responses can multiply tenfold.

Sense of Control

Complaining can provide individuals with a sense of control over their environment. In the workplace, many feel limited in their ability to influence their assignments or tasks, prompting them to complain as a means of asserting control. By vocalizing their dissatisfaction, they may feel they are taking action against the sources of their frustration, even if their circumstances remain unchanged.

Maintaining a positive outlook can be challenging, especially when frustrations or resentments about certain job aspects arise. Whenever possible, try to compartmentalize the elements of your job that annoy you the most. Focus on the tasks you enjoy and remind yourself that the rest is temporary.

In the meantime, boost your energy by listening to uplifting music. When stress feels overwhelming, step outside for a 15-minute walk. You might also consider journaling as a way to process your frustrations. Simply writing down (or typing) your thoughts and feelings can be cathartic. No one else needs to read it, so let the words flow freely. The goal is to discover productive ways to filter out your discontent and cultivate an inspirational, optimistic demeanor.

5. Build Your CREDIBILITY

Be the person on your team whom others can trust. This goes beyond your functional credibility regarding expertise and job skills; it encompasses your integrity and ability to foster strong working relationships.

Utilize the worksheet in Appendix F to assess how credible your peers perceive you to be.

1. Do your colleagues view you as someone they can count on?
    - Are you consistent in your actions and decisions?

Chapter Four: How To Create Instant and Sustainable Impact

- Do you follow through on commitments, even when faced with difficulties or inconveniences?

2. Do you keep your promises?
   - How often do you fulfill the commitments you make to your team?
   - Are you known for meeting deadlines and honoring agreements?

3. Do you live each day according to your values and morals?
   - Are your actions aligned with the ethical standards you profess to uphold?
   - Do you prioritize what is right over what is easy or personally advantageous?

4. Do you ever stretch the truth when it suits your needs?
   - Have you compromised your integrity to achieve short-term goals?
   - Are there instances where you justify bending the truth for personal gain?

5. How do you handle mistakes?
   - Do you take responsibility for your errors, or do you seek to deflect blame?
   - Are you transparent about your mistakes and proactive in finding solutions?

6. How do you respond to feedback?
   - Are you open to constructive criticism and willing to make necessary adjustments?
   - Do you actively seek feedback from peers to improve your performance?

7. Are you reliable in your communication?

- Do you communicate openly and honestly with your team?
- Are you timely in providing updates and responding to inquiries?

8. How do you support your team members?
   - Do you offer assistance to colleagues when they need it?
   - Are you willing to go the extra mile to ensure the team's success?

9. Do you respect confidentiality?
   - Can your team trust you with sensitive information?
   - Do you honor your colleagues' privacy and maintain professional discretion?

10. Are you consistent in your behavior?
    - Do you uphold the same ethical standards and behavior regardless of who is watching?
    - Are you a steady and dependable presence in the workplace?

11. How do you handle conflicts?
    - Do you address conflicts fairly with a focus on resolution?
    - Are you seen as a mediator who can be trusted to handle disputes impartially?

12. Do you demonstrate empathy and understanding?
    - Are you considerate of your colleagues' feelings and perspectives?
    - Do you show genuine concern for the well-being of others?

Reflecting on these questions can help you assess your trustworthiness and pinpoint areas for improvement. Building and maintaining trust is essential for creating a cohesive and effective team, beginning with individual accountability and integrity. To enhance your credibility, strive to demonstrate consistency in your attendance, participation, and work quality. Never compromise on standards of truth and honesty, and humbly take responsibility for your mistakes. Credible individuals are still human, so how you handle errors speaks volumes about your character. Your goal should be to be recognized as someone who "walks the walk and talks the talk."

6. Be THANKFUL

Make gratitude part of everything you do.

Leaders are drawn to employees who appreciate their blessings and refuse to take opportunities for granted. Trust us: the last individuals to be recognized or promoted are those who meander around the office with an irritating sense of entitlement and arrogance, believing they deserve more than they receive. (Pssst...Don't be that person.)

Start now and cultivate the habit of sincerely expressing your gratitude when entrusted with a special assignment, rewarded with a bonus, or provided with helpful feedback. Send a quick note or email to reiterate your thanks; it's a simple gesture that many people overlook.

Make thankfulness an integral part of your daily routine. You'll be amazed at how it transforms both you and those around you. We embrace daily gratitude to help us maintain a positive outlook. The 5-Minute Gratitude Plan can be found here: www.YouNextNow.com/5-MinuteGratitudePlan.

Making an IMPACT means recognizing that you have what it takes to position yourself for success. By following these steps and actions, you'll create the foundation you need to take charge of your life and career.

MAKE IT HAPPEN!

- Implement a plan to achieve immediate IMPACT while pursuing your professional development.
- Demonstrate INITIATIVE and passion for your work daily.
- Enhance your MARKETABILITY by aligning with corporate goals.
- Exude PROFESSIONALISM—verbally, nonverbally, and visually—to signal your readiness for promotion.
- Cultivate a positive ATTITUDE, even on the toughest days.
- Establish your CREDIBILITY by upholding high standards of honesty and integrity.
- Express THANKFULNESS for your career opportunities.

For more valuable tips, visit YouNextNow.com!

CHAPTER FIVE

ELEVATE
Your Leadership Skills

Olivia had been working at a packaged goods company for five years, proving herself to be a reliable and dedicated employee. Her department director could always count on her to complete tasks efficiently and effectively, without needing reminders or prodding.

Although Olivia had always dreamed of advancing within the organization, the prospect of making that leap felt daunting. As a hard-core introvert, she worried that her quiet nature might hinder her chances of promotion.

Finally, Olivia mustered the courage to discuss her goals (and fears) with her director. He reassured her that becoming a successful leader didn't require extreme extroversion; she simply needed to build her leadership skills and apply them within the framework of her natural personality. Would she still need to step out of her comfort zone? Absolutely. But Olivia began to contemplate how she could adapt her demeanor to become an effective entry-level manager.

Can you relate to Olivia? Perhaps you excel in your current role but struggle to exhibit the leadership traits necessary for promotion. This is a common challenge!

To get started, take the Leader's Blind Spot Assessment. It's quick and easy, designed to help you identify your superpowers and areas for improvement. Completing it takes less than five minutes, and many find it both interesting and enjoyable.

You can take the assessment here: www.productiveleaders.com/lbsa

> **Note:** This assessment requires your email address to send you your results.

There are thousands of books on building leadership skills. To avoid overwhelming you with information, we will focus on three key skill categories that can significantly enhance your visibility as a leader: strategic thinking, emotional intelligence, and confidence.

1. **Learn to be a strategic thinker.**

    Up until now, you've likely spent much of your time implementing strategies developed by others. Someone else has created the vision, while you've been tasked with executing the mission. Although this is a crucial aspect of the role, true leaders engage with the process from a different perspective. It's time to explore that new territory!

    While you may not be in a position to participate directly in broader discussions about overall corporate direction, you can still train your mind to think strategically. Consider the long-term impact of the decisions you make and their implications beyond your department or company. Use the SWOT analysis you probably learned in school: What are the strengths, weaknesses, opportunities, and threats associated with your choices?

Calculating every alternative from both short-term and long-term perspectives isn't always easy, but it's a skill you can develop with intention. Seek guidance from a mentor on how to strengthen this area. Practice consistently! Pay close attention to how great leaders tackle tough problems. By bringing a big-picture view to decision-making and team meetings, you'll showcase your abilities as a strategic leader ready to advance.

Example of Strategic Thinking

Imagine you are a manager at a mid-sized tech company facing rising competition. Your role involves overseeing the development of a new software product. Here's how you might approach this with strategic thinking:

1. **Swot Analysis:** Start by conducting a SWOT analysis to understand the internal and external factors that could impact your product's success.

    - *Strengths:* Your team has a robust background in software development, with several successful projects to its credit.
    - *Weaknesses:* Limited marketing resources and a relatively unknown brand in the market.
    - *Opportunities:* Growing demand for your type of software due to recent shifts in market trends.
    - *Threats:* Established competitors with larger budgets and greater market presence.

2. **Long-Term Vision:** Rather than just focusing on the immediate goal of launching the product, consider the long-term vision. What do you want the product to achieve in five years? Who will it serve? How will it align with the broader company strategy?

3. **Market Planning:** Develop various scenarios based on different market conditions and competitor actions. How would you respond if a major competitor released a similar product? What if there's an economic downturn? What if regulations affecting your industry were enacted?

4. **Resource Allocation:** Consider how to allocate resources not only for immediate tasks but also to build capabilities that will be beneficial in the long run. This may involve investing in marketing to enhance your brand or developing partnerships that can create new market opportunities.

5. **Engage Stakeholders:** Ensure you engage stakeholders from different areas of the company to gather their input and gain buy-in. This could involve discussions with marketing, sales, and customer support teams to understand their perspectives and incorporate their insights into your strategy.

By adopting a strategic mindset for your project, you not only enhance the likelihood of your product's success but also showcase your ability to think and act like a strategic leader. This positions you favorably for future leadership roles and responsibilities.

Strategic thinkers apply key characteristics in their workplaces and leverage their strategies to advance projects effectively.

Strategic Thinking at Work

Consider a marketing director at a consumer goods company tasked with launching a new product. Here's how they might demonstrate strategic thinking:

- **Visionary:** They set a goal for the new product to capture 20% of the market share within two years. While setting such a goal is straightforward, the critical step is selecting specific actions to achieve it, such as:
- **Analytical Skills:** They analyze market research to understand customer preferences and identify potential competitors.
- **Creative Problem-Solving:** They devise a unique marketing campaign that differentiates the product from its competitors.
- **Forward-Thinking:** They plan for potential supply chain disruptions and establish backup suppliers.
- **Adaptability:** They modify the marketing strategy based on early sales data and customer feedback.
- **Decisiveness:** They swiftly decide to increase the marketing budget upon observing positive initial sales. Strike while the iron is hot!
- **Holistic Perspective:** They consider how the new product will affect the company's existing product lines and overall brand image.
- **Effective Communication:** They clearly convey the product launch plan to the sales team and other stakeholders.
- **Collaboration:** They work closely with the product development team, sales team, and external partners to ensure a successful launch.
- **Continuous Learning:** They attend industry conferences and read market reports to stay informed about the latest trends.

- **Risk Management:** They conduct a risk assessment and develop contingency plans for potential challenges.
- **Customer Focus:** They prioritize features and benefits that meet customer needs, ensuring high customer satisfaction.

By embodying these characteristics, the marketing director not only drives the successful launch of the new product but also positions themselves as a strategic leader within the organization.

1. **Increase your emotional intelligence.**

We've discussed extensively in this book the importance of talents, skills, education, and experience. Emotional intelligence is the glue that binds all these elements together. It encompasses the intangible qualities that differentiate a polished, influential professional from a character like Sheldon Cooper on The Big Bang Theory. The key takeaway is that knowledge alone does not make you an exceptional leader.

So, what does it truly mean to be emotionally intelligent? For one, it involves possessing excellent self-awareness. The better you understand yourself—the good, the bad, and the areas in progress—the greater your chances of becoming a respected leader.

Self-aware individuals can accurately assess the impact they have on others and know how to "read a room." Their interpersonal skills are exceptional, allowing them to build strong relationships. They are sensitive to the needs of others and can comfortably express empathy. They manage stress effectively and remain calm in crises, quickly bouncing back after challenging times.

What are some key components of individuals with high emotional intelligence?

Rate yourself on a scale of 1 (low) to 5 (high) in these areas.

1. **Self-Awareness.** Understanding your own emotions, strengths, weaknesses, values, and motives is essential. Are you honest with yourself and others? Can you reflect on your behavior and its impact?

    1   2   3   4   5

2. **Self-Regulation.** The ability to control or redirect disruptive emotions and impulses is crucial. Do you remain calm and composed in stressful situations? Are you able to adapt to change?

    1   2   3   4   5

3. **Motivation.** Being driven by a desire to achieve for its own sake is essential. Are you motivated by a passion for your work and the new challenges it presents, rather than just external rewards like money or status?

    1   2   3   4   5

4. **Empathy.** The ability to understand the emotional issues of others is crucial. Can you empathize with someone else's perspective and respond with care and understanding?

    1   2   3   4   5

5. **Social Skills**: Proficiency in managing relationships and building networks is essential. Are you able to communicate

effectively, resolve conflicts, inspire others, and collaborate effectively in a team setting?

1   2   3   4   5

If you are looking to actively improve your emotional intelligence, consider how Joshua employed these emotional intelligence strategies to effectively lead his team through a challenging multinational project.

- **Self-Awareness:** Joshua recognized a tense moment when both he and the team felt overwhelmed. He announced a break to allow everyone to regain their composure before addressing and refocusing the team.
- **Self-Regulation:** During a heated discussion, Joshua facilitated the conversation in a way that kept everyone calm and composed, guiding it toward a constructive resolution.
- **Motivation:** Joshua inspired the team with his passion for the project. He set clear, achievable goals to keep everyone motivated and ensured that deadlines were communicated weekly so that everyone stayed informed and on track.
- **Empathy:** Joshua noticed that Frank was struggling with a lack of focus, which turned out to be due to a personal health issue. Joshua offered support and flexibility to help Frank adjust his schedule for medical appointments while managing his workload.
- **Social Skills:** Joshua held frequent meetings with the team to encourage collaboration, foster camaraderie, and effectively mediate issues that arose during the project. Remember, not every meeting has to last an hour!

By actively demonstrating these characteristics, Joshua not only successfully navigated the project but also built a strong, cohesive team that trusted and respected his leadership.

2. Boost your confidence.

If you want to be seen as a leader, you must act like one and feel like one. The only way to achieve this is to boost your confidence.

Why is that? In our fast-paced world, there's no business playbook that defines exactly what we should be doing. The rules change constantly. It takes highly confident individuals to navigate this challenging landscape.

The most successful leaders today possess the confidence to maneuver through uncertainty. They are willing to move forward and take calculated risks. They are bold enough to develop plans despite numerous unknowns. They believe in their ideas and have the power to inspire others to support their decisions. Perhaps most importantly, they hold themselves accountable for the outcomes—both positive and negative—recognizing that they can course-correct as needed to improve results over time.

If you want to be perceived as a confident, leadership-ready professional, here are some characteristics you should project:

- Self-motivation
- Passion
- Optimism
- Courage
- Decisiveness
- Flexibility
- Responsibility
- Dependability
- Accountability
- Humility
- Transparency
- Reliability

That all sounds great, but you might be wondering how to incorporate these characteristics.

Remember, confident individuals gain their strength from facing their fears and ultimately succeeding. In other words, their desire to acquire new skills outweighs the fear associated with trying them.

Confidence is built through action.

As you begin to cultivate your confidence, start small. Identify something that intimidates you or that you've been hesitant to try. This could be skydiving, learning to play the guitar, or taking a finance class. Whatever it is, choose something that elicits a healthy level of anxiety. Give it a try, and push through the fear. No pressure—you're not aiming to become the world's greatest skydiver, Jack White, or Warren Buffett. Just focus on getting through the experience.

The goal is to tackle and complete something that seems hard, scary, or uncomfortable. When you achieve that goal, celebrate your victory! Then try something else. Through this ongoing process, you'll start to see yourself as the kind of person who acknowledges the fear of a new experience or situation and keeps moving through it. No matter what happens, you'll figure it out. You've done it before; you'll do it again.

That's confidence in bloom, folks!

Fast-forward a couple of years. (Fill in your own confidence boosters in the next sentence!) Imagine your skydiving, guitar-playing, financially savvy self receiving the news that your employer is filing for bankruptcy. Or being selected to make a presentation to the CEO the day after tomorrow. Or losing your biggest client.

All of these qualify as heart-palpitating, sweaty-palm events. However, you've faced your fears in the past and always emerged intact. This, too, is a mountain you can climb.

Whatever challenge comes your way, you have the confidence to manage it and devise a workable plan. Sure, that plan might not be perfect, but you also know you can think on your feet and adapt as needed. If necessary, you have the confidence to admit you need help. You can take responsibility for bringing in someone with the expertise to get the job done.

The cumulative effect is remarkable. Big challenge? Bring it on. You've got this!

When you have the confidence to tackle difficult tasks, you'll automatically project a wide array of leadership qualities that will capture attention. The key takeaway? Confidence is the gateway to leadership.

Start your journey to becoming a better leader by taking the Leader's Blind Spot Assessment. Use the strategic characteristics to identify areas for growth. Enhance your emotional intelligence by applying those traits in daily situations. Remember that regularly facing fears builds resilience and adaptability. Confident individuals can manage unexpected challenges and naturally project leadership qualities.

Here are some of our favorite leadership books that may be helpful:

The Competent Leader by Peter Stark and Jane Flaherty

Master Your World by Mary Kelly

Thrive by Meridith Elliott Powell

MAKE IT HAPPEN!

- Complete the Leader's Blind Spot Assessment at: https://productiveleaders.com/leadersbsassessment/
- Enhance your leadership skills to showcase your readiness for advancement.
- Engage in strategic thinking while considering overall corporate objectives.
- Strengthen your emotional intelligence and self-awareness.
- Boost your confidence by consistently challenging yourself to tackle difficult problems. Establish your CREDIBILITY by upholding high standards of honesty and integrity.
- Express THANKFULNESS for your career opportunities.

For more valuable tips, visit YouNextNow.com!

CHAPTER SIX

BE A
Team Player

When Robert accepted a job offer from a growing software company, the CEO felt as though he had won the high-tech lottery. Robert was essentially an IT genius and added immense value during his first two years with the organization. The executive team was eager to keep him happy and challenged. However, when Robert approached his supervisor about opportunities for advancement within the company, she had some reservations.

The problem? Although Robert got along relatively well with his peers, he strongly preferred to work independently. Collaborating with others was noticeably frustrating for him—likely because his brain operated at a significantly different pace. Nevertheless, his manager needed to address the issue. Despite his technical brilliance, Robert couldn't advance within the organization unless he became more successful at being a team player.

That's a deal-breaker.

Whether you're a rocket scientist or a rock star, you cannot advance in your career without being part of a team. It's simply not feasible. Organizations of all sizes complete tasks through both internal and external teams. ("Two heads are better than one" may be a tired cliché, but it remains relevant!) If you aspire to be a highly valued employee on the fast track, you must elevate your game in terms of being a team player.

 Think about your experiences with working on teams in the last few years. How would you characterize the role you typically played in your team meetings?

Choose from the list below or add one of your own.

- I organized everything and prepared the agenda.
- I was the creative idea person most involved in brainstorming.
- I handled logistics and compliance.
- I took notes and updated the status reports.
- I completed the majority of the work because others didn't finish their assignments.
- I used meetings as an opportunity to voice my opinions and share my perspectives.
- I mostly listened and processed the information being shared.
- I found myself bored, counting down the minutes until the meetings ended.
- I was just there for the bagels and coffee.

All kidding aside, take a moment to consider whether your typical role as a team member might have been a factor that worked against you when you were evaluated for advancement. Awkward, right?

It's not uncommon for ambitious professionals to focus more on refining their individual contributions than on their team participation. This is a natural response, as many feel a sense of competition when vying for the next promotion, often seeing their peers in the same team meetings as their main competitors. This can create a mental challenge.

But here's the truth: your career will not succeed if you don't master the art of working on a team. There's no gray area and no room for discussion—this is a cold, hard fact. So, if you've spent more time concentrating on "me" rather than "we," here are three things you can do to become a world-class team member—someone who helps the group generate results and is ready to play at a higher level.

1. Embrace the group dynamic.

You can't avoid working as a group, so it's time to change the way you think about it. If you've been subconsciously viewing your teammates as competitors or, ahem, less qualified participants, it's time to reframe that perspective. You're all on the same side, united by a common goal.

That was Robert's challenge. He needed to stop seeing his teammates as a drag on his productivity or as people who didn't fully appreciate his groundbreaking ideas. While they might not match his technical expertise, he needed to recognize the different kinds of value his teammates could contribute.

When teams are properly organized, they bring together individuals with diverse ideas and complementary strengths. This design enhances the potential for powerful synergy, creative ideas, and bold decision-making. If Robert wanted to accelerate his career path, he would have to slow down enough to tap into the unique yet equally valuable assets of his teammates. Their areas of expertise might be exactly what he needs to showcase his high-tech innovations more profitably.

When you shift your attitude and embrace the potential of teamwork, you'll become more open to shared problem-solving and the bigger results it can produce. Even better? Collaborative thinking could become your competitive advantage.

2. Leverage opportunities for growth.

Participating on a team offers a wide range of opportunities to develop the exact skills you'll need for a higher leadership position. By focusing on these opportunities, you'll gain significant on-the-job professional development.

Need some examples?

As a future senior leader, you'll need to prioritize the collective benefits of the group rather than operate within your individual silo. You can start practicing this mindset right now as a team member.

Consider ways to enhance your team's effectiveness, such as supporting and inspiring others, strengthening relationships, and building trust. By seeking out and seizing these opportunities, you'll cultivate important leadership qualities that will set you apart from the crowd.

Team interactions can serve as an ideal classroom for expanding your self-awareness. Pay close attention to how your words, actions, and attitudes impact others in your group. Are you striving to understand their perspectives, or are you more focused on "selling" your own suggestions? Challenge yourself to pause and remain open to the unique views of others regarding a challenge. What motivates them? What's most important to them? Why?

Your communication skills will also be put to the test as you express your ideas and opinions clearly, concisely, and persuasively. How effectively do you handle conflict resolution? You may have

Chapter Six: Be A Player

opportunities to practice this skill as well! If a group discussion veers off course, position yourself as the calm voice of reason to refocus the conversation on the primary goals. Notice if anyone is left out of the discussion and gently invite them to share their thoughts.

Even if you're not an official team leader at this moment, you can use your experience working within a group to prepare for that role as your career progresses.

3. Share the credit <u>and</u> the burden.

One hallmark of a great team player is the ability to generously share credit for the group's success. The lesson for you? Don't put yourself in the spotlight after a team win, and refrain from pointing fingers when something goes wrong. Win or lose, it's a team event.

> Openly giving credit to others will earn you plenty of respect and increase your professional reputation.

Naturally, there's some fine print that accompanies that statement. While it might feel counterintuitive to those with a competitive mindset, be the first to congratulate someone on your team for a great idea or smart solution. Even better, tell others about that person's pivotal contributions. Not only will this give them a well-deserved boost, but you'll also reap the rewards. Openly giving credit to others will earn you plenty of respect and increase your professional reputation.

No, the fine print doesn't include an option for the reverse situation. This should probably go without saying, but we'll say it anyway: If your team suffers an epic loss, you can investigate the problem without openly placing blame. Avoid gossip or disparaging remarks about a teammate. While Joe might have totally dropped the ball, vocally criticizing him will reflect poorly on you—and not in a positive way.

You Next

Part of sharing both the credit and the burden with your team means preserving and strengthening relationships with your teammates. Regardless of what happened in the past, those connections will be vital for working on your next project and, hopefully, achieving your next win.

If you can excel in your role as a team player, you'll increase your value to the organization and build a professional reputation as someone who is prepared for promotion.

MAKE IT HAPPEN!

- ➢ Enhance your value by collaborating effectively as part of a team.
- ➢ Embrace the group dynamic to harness the power of collaborative thinking.
- ➢ Capitalize on opportunities for growth within the team setting.
- ➢ Share both the credit and the burden graciously with your team members.

For more valuable tips, visit YouNextNow.com!

CHAPTER SEVEN

EXPAND
Your Network

A young woman named Sharon took a job as a bank clerk, knowing she wanted more but having no idea how to build a career or move beyond her current role. Everything changed when she volunteered to help her boss with an unusual project, learning a vital skill every professional needs to change the trajectory of their life and career.

Sharon worked for an older woman who not only managed her but also owned the company. Well into her late seventies when Sharon joined the firm, this woman was sharp, hardworking, and had built the business from the ground up. A true trailblazer, she faced a challenge: due to vision loss, she could no longer drive herself to work or attend the early morning church services she cherished.

When Sharon learned of her boss's dilemma, she offered to help. Healthy, single, and without morning commitments, she was happy to rise early and assist, even though she wasn't a churchgoer.

You Next

To her surprise, Sharon found that she genuinely enjoyed attending church services. The pastor was engaging, and the community was welcoming. She loved it so much that she began attending on her own and volunteering for special events.

After a year, Sharon had developed a strong network and became active on several committees. One day, she received a call from the church pastor inviting her to join a new committee. Always eager to volunteer, Sharon said yes without knowing its purpose. The church was growing, and they needed to discuss raising funds for a new building. Although unsure of what to expect, Sharon felt ready for the challenge.

At her first meeting, Sharon entered a room filled with some of the most powerful and influential leaders in the church, community, and state. This gathering represented a wealth of knowledge, skills, and contacts—an opportunity to expand her network. Feeling intimidated, she asked her pastor if he had made a mistake in inviting her. Laughing, he assured her he hadn't, explaining that her ability to build relationships, coupled with her commitment and selflessness, made her just as deserving as those leaders.

Sharon connected with some of the most important professionals in her state. If she hadn't been willing to drive her boss to church, join committees, and form relationships, she would have missed out on these invaluable connections. Over the years, Sharon continued to cultivate relationships with these movers and shakers, showcasing her skills and talents. She discovered that every time she offered to serve and help others, she created more valuable connections. While not her initial motivation, volunteering opened countless doors.

Today, Sharon runs one of the most prestigious financial services firms in the Southeast, attributing her success to the connections made through the church.

The most successful individuals are those with the strongest networks. By building your network, you can transform your life and career. The more you invest in nurturing your network, the more it will nurture your life and career in return.

Networking can be intimidating. We understand that walking into a room full of strangers and starting conversations can be daunting. On her first day at church, Sharon was nervous but took a deep breath and made the leap. Her courage paid off.

While we cannot eliminate the awkwardness of networking, we can assure you that it offers one of the strongest returns on investment if you're willing to step outside your comfort zone.

> If you study successful people, one thing you will see they have in common is that they invest in building relationships and connections long before they need them.

Whether you feel your career is stagnating or you simply want more control over your future, one of the best strategies is to build and expand your network. In today's marketplace, it's often more about "who you know" than "what you know." While this may spark debate, many—including Sharon—would wholeheartedly agree.

Here are six effective strategies to expand your connections and significantly enhance your career.

1. Learn to network properly.

One reason we often hesitate to network is that we have never been taught how to do it. Think about it: your mother likely advised you not to talk to strangers.

From the very beginning, we've been conditioned to view conversations with people we don't know as something negative. It's no wonder we feel uncomfortable when it comes to networking.

If you study successful people, one thing you will see they have in common is that they invest in building relationships and connections long before they need them.

Networking is a lifestyle, not just a task.

So how do you network effectively?

Understand that networking is not about you. Many people hesitate to network because they dislike talking about themselves, feel unsure of what to say, or don't know how to respond to questions. Here's the good news: networking is not about you. Your goal is to learn about others. Aim to talk 20 percent of the time and let others talk 80 percent of the time.

At networking events, asking thoughtful and engaging questions can help break the ice and build meaningful connections.

Here are some networking questions designed to foster genuine conversation and curiosity:

a. Opening Questions

- "What brought you to this event today?"
  This friendly question helps you start a conversation and learn more about their purpose for attending.

- "How did you hear about this event?"
  This question can help you find common ground or mutual acquaintances.

- "Is there something you're hoping to learn from today's event?"
  Encouraging them to share their goals allows you to see if there are ways you can support them or connect them with someone who can.

b. Professional Curiosity

- "Do you have any exciting projects that you are currently working on?"
  This helps you understand their current interests, which could lead to collaborative opportunities.

- "What's challenging in your role right now?"
  This question opens the door for a deeper conversation about industry trends, personal growth, or professional challenges.

- "What do you enjoy about your industry?"
  Industry-related questions are non-threatening and encourage them to share what they like about their work.

c. Industry Insights

- "What trends are you noticing in your industry right now?"
  This shows your interest in their professional perspective and can lead to a deeper discussion on industry knowledge.

- "If you could give one piece of advice to someone starting in your field, what would it be?"
  You might preface this with, "My nephew is interested in that field." This shows respect for their experience.

- "What do you think are the next big changes for your industry?"
  This demonstrates that you're forward-thinking and interested in strategic conversations.

d. Event-Specific

- "Have you been to any other events like this before?"
  This could lead to a conversation about mutual events, interests, or people.

- "What's been the most interesting thing you've learned at this event so far?"

This question helps to share knowledge and exchange insights gained from the event.

- "Is there anyone here I can introduce you to?"
  You may find opportunities to introduce them to someone you know or share common interests.

Nurture the relationships you cultivate. Once you meet and engage with people, identify those you are most interested in or have the most in common with, and continue to nurture those connections.

Invest in others before asking for their investment in you. Always prioritize giving and supporting others before seeking anything in return.

2. Build your internal network.

Begin by compiling a list of the top ten individuals within your company or industry who would be considered valuable connections. Which relationships are essential for helping you perform your job more effectively?

These individuals might include the CEO of your company, the VP of Operations, the IT Director, a department manager, a remarkably creative co-worker, the President of your industry organization, or even a trusted colleague at a competing firm.

To assist you in creating your list, consider the following qualifying questions:

- Which individuals within your company or industry directly impact your ability to succeed?
- Which individuals within your company or industry indirectly influence your success?

- Who is highly respected, influential, and well-connected within your company or industry?
- Who do you admire for their outstanding work ethic and impressive achievements?
- Who has previously succeeded in your current role, as well as in the role you aspire to?

In many cases, you may already have relationships with some of these individuals. The goal here is to make these connections more strategic and intentional. By proactively building and maintaining your internal network, you can establish a solid foundation of essential support across the most critical areas of your company and industry.

3. Strengthen your external connections.

The next step is to think beyond the immediate bubble of your organization. Create a list of your top ten clients, your top ten referral sources, and your top ten community leaders. Community leaders might include an executive from your Chamber of Commerce, a board member from a local business club, or a government official.

To guide your thinking about relationships that could add value to your career, consider the following qualifying questions:

- Which clients generate the most revenue for my company?
- Have I developed relationships with any of these clients that go beyond transactions?
- How did I originally acquire leads for these clients?
- What other referral sources have resulted in successful clients or projects? (Consider existing clients, strategic partners, vendors, neighbors, friends, and family.)

- Has community involvement or visibility produced tangible business advantages for me? (Such as new customers, unexpected information sources, or preferential treatment.)
- Which individuals within the community would be valuable partners to help develop or expand those advantages?

Even when your calendar is overflowing, it's essential to stay connected with these individuals who have the power to impact your success. Check in regularly and maintain contact, offering to help whenever you can—even unsolicited. This style of targeted networking is one of the most effective ways to build your professional reputation and will undoubtedly yield a strong return on investment for your career

4. Increase your resources.

No matter how smart and talented we are, we can't excel at everything. It's simply not possible. Fortunately, we don't have to be. Instead, we need to know others who are ready and willing to fill in the gaps. By fortifying these relationships, we can create an unstoppable synergy that positions us for greater success.

Consider this analogy: if you were stranded on a deserted island with two other people, your outlook would be much brighter if each person brought unique skills to the table. Your chances of survival increase if one person knows how to fish, another can build a sturdy shelter, and the third is knowledgeable about plants. Together, you'll last much longer than if all three of you were just carpenters. That's the essence of collaboration.

Surrounding yourself with people who possess contrasting skills and talents can build a resource network that significantly enhances your success. You might need access to an innovative thinker, a visionary strategic planner, a technology guru, an exceptional project manager, or someone who is politically connected. Take the time to find the right individuals.

To help identify the best people for your resource network, consider these questions:

- What skills (beyond your own) are necessary for you to achieve greater success?
- Who do you know that possesses these skills and applies them at a high level?
- If you could hire three consultants to support your efforts, whom would you choose?
- Who would you want in your corner if you faced a significant challenge?
- What skills do they possess? Do you know others with similar capabilities?

While it may be easier to connect with people who share similar backgrounds and interests, resist that tendency. Instead, stretch yourself to make connections with individuals who can offer diverse perspectives and skills to your resource network.

5. Develop a support system.

When we typically discuss networking, the emphasis often focuses on reaching out. However, a crucial aspect of career development involves finding the right people who can reach in and support you on a more personal level. These connections can provide the wisdom and encouragement that become the catalysts for meteoric success.

Here are four options to consider as you develop a support system to help sustain your career:

- Mentor: Identify a few individuals, typically those older than you, who have forged career paths you admire. Get to know them and see if a potential mentoring relationship develops. It may take time to find someone who aligns with your skill sets, temperament, and commitment. However, once you discover a mentor you trust and who believes in you, that relationship can become one of your most valuable career assets.

  A crucial footnote: While you seek their advice and guidance, make it a two-way street. Actively find ways to add value for your mentors and present them with new opportunities as well.

  (See Appendix G for a list of mentorship questions you can use to connect with and learn from your mentor.)

- Coach: At certain points in your life, investing in a career coach can be beneficial. A coach can help you assess your situation and develop objective solutions, particularly as you navigate career challenges and obstacles to advancement.

- Accountability Partner: Partner with a peer who also has career objectives they want to achieve. Share your goals and challenges, then hold each other accountable to make progress and achieve success.

- Selected Family Members and Friends: Consider who genuinely cares about you and takes an interest in your well-being. These are the people who will steadfastly support you, whether you receive the promotion or struggle with a presentation. As you work diligently to advance your career, make sure to devote time to nurturing these relationships; they are essential for your mental and emotional health!

Chapter Seven: Expand Your Network

We want to emphasize that networking to build real, meaningful relationships is critical for both your career and happiness. Having the right people to advise, guide, and support you increases your overall opportunities and ultimately helps build your career.

MAKE IT HAPPEN!

- ➤ Expand Your Professional Network: Strengthen your career by actively building relationships with a diverse range of professionals.
- ➤ Foster Connections Within Your Organization: Cultivate meaningful connections with colleagues at all levels to enhance collaboration and visibility.
- ➤ Make Strategic Contacts Across Your Industry: Develop relationships with key players in your industry, community, and the broader business world to open new opportunities.
- ➤ Create a Diverse Resource Network: Surround yourself with individuals who possess different skills and talents, enhancing your ability to tackle challenges and innovate.
- ➤ Establish a Strong Support System: Build a network that includes a mentor, a coach, an accountability partner, and supportive friends and family to guide and motivate you throughout your career journey.

For more valuable tips, visit YouNextNow.com!

CHAPTER EIGHT

MAKE
Yourself Invaluable

Maggie landed a job with a top accounting firm right after finishing her MBA. She knows how to work hard and gives 100% every day. Putting herself through college at her state school, she loved the idea of working at one of the top accounting firms in the U.S.

From day one, Maggie knew she wanted to get promoted and move up through the organization faster than anyone else her age, and she had a plan. Ruth, one of the company's senior vice presidents, recognized Maggie's spunky, hard-working style and soon became her mentor.

In one of their meetings, Maggie presented Ruth with an exhaustive list of all the career development activities she was pursuing. She had signed up for several conferences, volunteered to work at the firm's job fair booth, and was taking a self-paced online course to develop her leadership skills. Additionally, she became a committee chair for the local trade association.

Ruth was truly impressed by Maggie's drive and energy, applauding all her efforts. But she also offered Maggie some priceless advice:

"Sometimes the formula for getting promoted is simpler than you think. Just find a way to make yourself the employee that the company wants to keep—and can't afford to lose."

Maggie was doing all the right things, but her shotgun approach to career advancement wasn't yielding the immediate results she wanted. It was time to become laser-focused on her true career aspirations.

Many of the people we work with have a solid understanding of all the pieces in the career development puzzle. They know what to do, but like Maggie, they fall a little short in the one category that truly matters for getting promoted.

ASK YOURSELF?

- Am I an invaluable, indispensable asset that the company needs for its future success?
- If that is not yet recognized, how can I prove my worth and become someone others rely on?
- How do I become the go-to person?
- What skills do I possess that this company needs?

Chapter Eight: Make Yourself Invaluable

SEVEN ROLES YOU CAN PLAY WITHIN YOUR ORGANIZATION

We want to share seven different roles you can adopt within your organization to position yourself as a must-have, value-added team member. There are many more, but these are some of the most common.

1. The Expert

You can open doors to new opportunities, career advancement, and industry recognition by distinguishing yourself as an expert in your field. Whether you're just starting your career or looking to elevate your professional standing, becoming a subject matter expert is a strategic path that requires dedication, continuous learning, and effective communication.

The path of the expert is not trivial—enter it only after careful thought. Choose your area of expertise with caution; no one wants to consult the second-best expert in any field.

Work to become the person within your company that others rely on when they need help in a specific area. Freely share your knowledge and encourage colleagues to reach out if they require additional assistance.

You can become a subject matter expert who knows everything there is to know about a particular topic in your industry. You understand its history, current status, and upcoming trends. You also grasp how the industry and your competitors are approaching the subject, positioning yourself as a recognized thought leader in that area.

For some, expertise involves staying updated with technology and tools that enable faster, more efficient work. Commit to studying the latest tech trends, learning new skills rapidly, and helping colleagues incorporate technology to improve their productivity.

You Next

Here's how you can position yourself as the go-to person within your company and industry:

Identify Your Area of Expertise

The first step in becoming an expert is to identify the area in which you want to excel. This could be a specific technology, a particular aspect of your industry, or a skill that is highly valued in your field.

- **Assess Your Interests:** Choose an area that genuinely excites you, as passion fuels motivation and persistence.
- **Evaluate Your Organization's Needs:** Align your expertise with industry trends and demands to ensure that it remains relevant and valuable.
- **Leverage Your Strengths:** Build on your existing skills and knowledge to accelerate your journey toward expertise.

Develop Deep Knowledge

Once you've identified your niche, commit to becoming an authority in that area. This involves gaining a comprehensive understanding of your chosen subject, including its history, current trends, and future outlook.

- **Continuous Learning:** Regularly engage in courses, workshops, and webinars to keep your skills sharp and your knowledge up-to-date.
- **Stay Informed:** Subscribe to industry publications, podcasts, and newsletters to remain aware of the latest developments and insights.
- **Research and Analysis:** Conduct your own research and analyze industry reports to gain a deeper understanding of your field. Don't forget to examine what your competition is publishing!

Share Your Expertise

Being an expert is not just about possessing knowledge; it's also about sharing it effectively with others. Communicate your insights and ideas in a way that is accessible and valuable to your colleagues and peers.

- Coaching: Offer to coach junior colleagues or team members, helping them navigate challenges and improve their skills. You never learn as much as when you teach someone else!

- Create Content: Write articles, create videos, or host webinars that showcase your expertise and provide valuable insights. Even if these remain within your organization, you will establish yourself as an expert.

- Discuss Your Topic with Other Experts: Participate in industry forums, social media discussions, and networking events to share your knowledge and learn from others.

Leverage Technology

Stay updated on technology to drive efficiency and innovation in today's fast-paced work environment. Embrace new tools and platforms to enhance your productivity and support your role as an expert.

Use technology to measure the impact of your expertise on your team and organization. This will not only validate your efforts but also highlight areas for further growth and development. Regularly seek feedback from peers and supervisors to understand how your expertise is perceived and how it can be improved.

Becoming a subject matter expert is a journey that requires ongoing commitment, adaptability, and a genuine desire to add value to your organization and industry.

Balance being a helpful provider of information and advice with avoiding the pitfall of becoming a know-it-all who makes others feel inferior. When you assist others, be kind and generous to foster goodwill and avoid creating resentment.

2. *The Idea Generator*

If you are naturally creative and know how to approach problems in fresh ways, you may have found your niche in the organization as the Idea Generator. Most people eventually get stuck in a rut, doing things the same way they always have or viewing them from the same angle. In today's competitive global marketplace, innovation is one of the few differentiators that organizations can leverage. You can use this to your advantage in your career.

The Idea Generator role is often ideal for a young person or someone who has recently joined the company. Questions are among the most valuable contributions a new employee can bring, such as:

- "Why do you do it that way?"
- "Why don't you try X?"

When senior employees confront a problem, they often compare it to their past experiences: "This looks similar to the problem we had six years ago, and we did X back then." This tendency, while rarely verbalized, can stifle innovation. However, no improvement is possible if we keep relying on old standard solutions. Simply asking "why" and "why not" can help break the shackles of tradition and encourage senior employees to view the situation with fresh eyes.

Play an active role in brainstorming sessions and be the person who helps the team push the envelope when appropriate. If you sense that a project is slipping into cookie-cutter mode, speak up! Share viable alternatives along with solid rationale for your choices. Take the time to study how other companies in your industry (or beyond) are implementing unconventional processes or introducing revolutionary products.

To stimulate more discussion or to find alternative ideas, consider asking "what if?" questions, such as:

- What if we changed this approach?
- What if we stopped producing this way?
- What if we partnered with a different distributor?
- What if we changed working hours?

As people become more comfortable with the possibility of new ideas, you can present bolder suggestions, such as:

- What if we shifted our marketing focus from Asia to Europe to take advantage of the increased tourism in that area?
- What if we changed how our sales teams process orders?
- What if we created our own distribution center?
- What if we asked our teams what days and hours they want to work?
- While some individuals may struggle with new ideas, decision-makers are actively seeking people who think innovatively.

When you can consistently lead outside-the-box thinking, you'll be recognized as a valuable resource.

3. The Solution Finder

Every company faces its fair share of complex challenges, and top management often announces a game plan to address them. One way to distinguish yourself is to push yourself to think of better alternatives. Is there a different strategy that could resolve the issue faster or reduce expenses? Every organization needs a reliable Solution Finder to come up with unique approaches or intelligent shortcuts.

Be a resourceful strategic thinker who considers the short- and long-term impacts of decisions, as well as financial implications, staffing requirements, and branding issues. By developing a reputation as the team member who embodies the spirit of "where there's a will, there's a way," you'll be solidifying your future success.

4. The Efficiency Guru

For teams to maximize their productivity, they must operate both efficiently and effectively. This means not only completing tasks but also doing so in a manner that minimizes waste and optimizes resources.

Professionals who excel at fostering efficiency are often regarded as top performers and key contributors to their organizations. If you feel that this is a skill that resonates with you, consider stepping up your game to lead by example.

Here are some specific ways you can become a catalyst for efficiency within your team and organization:

- **Lead by example.** The most effective way to encourage efficiency in others is to embody it yourself. By demonstrating a strong work ethic, commitment to deadlines, and attention to detail, you set a standard for your colleagues to follow.

- **Hold yourself accountable for projects and deadlines.** This means not only meeting deadlines but also consistently delivering high-quality work. By showing that you are reliable and disciplined, you inspire others to uphold the same standards.

- **Practice excellent time management.** Prioritize tasks and avoid procrastination. Use tools such as calendars and task lists to organize your workload and ensure that you are working on the most important tasks at the right time. If you

Chapter Eight: Make Yourself Invaluable

need additional resources on how to reclaim your time and stop procrastinating, see the "Stop Procrastinating Tomorrow Workbook Summary" in Appendix H.

Bonus: There is a link to the full workbook as well.

- **Streamline processes.** Efficiency often comes down to how well processes are designed and executed. By streamlining workflows and eliminating unnecessary steps, you can help your team work more efficiently.
    - Are there any redundant steps that could be eliminated?
    - Could certain tasks be automated to save time and effort?
    - What tasks can be outsourced?
- **Implement strategic workarounds.** Despite the best-laid plans, unexpected challenges can arise that threaten to derail progress. Implementing strategic workarounds can help your team stay on track and maintain efficiency even in the face of obstacles.
- **Outsourcing:** Consider outsourcing portions of a project when internal resources are stretched thin. This can be an effective way to meet deadlines and maintain quality without overburdening your team.
- **Flexible Solutions:** Be open to flexible solutions that accommodate changing circumstances. This might involve adjusting timelines, reallocating resources, or finding alternative methods to achieve the same results.
- **Resilience Planning**: Develop resilience plans that outline potential scenarios and contingency measures. By preparing for the unexpected, your team can respond swiftly and effectively, minimizing disruptions to productivity.

Cultivate a culture of efficiency.

Ultimately, creating a culture that values efficiency involves fostering an environment where everyone is committed to working smarter, not harder. Recognize and reward team members who demonstrate exceptional efficiency and contribute to the overall productivity of the group. This practice reinforces positive behavior and motivates others to strive for similar achievements.

Efficiency is not just about working faster; it's about working smarter and making the best use of available resources to achieve optimal outcomes.

5. The Relationship Builder

A company's success isn't solely measured by its revenue. Many of the world's greatest brands have achieved their status by building solid relationships—with customers, employees, suppliers, and communities. If you thrive in a relationship-building capacity, your company needs those skills now more than ever.

Position Yourself as a Trusted Advisor

One key aspect of relationship-building is positioning yourself as a trusted advisor to your customers and an ambassador for your company throughout the industry and beyond. This involves not only understanding your clients' needs but also anticipating them and providing solutions that resonate with their goals. Being a trusted advisor requires consistency, transparency, and reliability in your dealings.

Howard Schultz, the former CEO of Starbucks, exemplifies a leader who excelled in relationship-building. Schultz transformed Starbucks into a global brand by focusing on creating a welcoming environment for customers and employees alike. He emphasized the importance of personal connections between baristas and customers, encouraging employees to remember regular customers' names and orders. Schultz's ability to connect with people on a personal level helped Starbucks maintain a loyal customer base and fostered a strong company culture.

Chapter Eight: Make Yourself Invaluable

Build Strong Partnerships

Building strong partnerships involves more than just transactional relationships; it requires nurturing long-term connections with internal teams, suppliers, and other stakeholders. Being a good partner means forging bonds based on trust, mutual respect, and shared goals.

Richard Branson, the founder of the Virgin Group, is renowned for his exceptional ability to connect with people and build strong partnerships. Branson's approach to business emphasizes valuing employees and partners. He famously said, "Clients do not come first. Employees come first. If you take care of your employees, they will take care of the clients." By prioritizing his employees and fostering a sense of belonging, Branson has created a network of loyal partners and employees committed to the Virgin brand's success.

Enhance Communication Skills and Emotional Intelligence

Effective communication and emotional intelligence are crucial components of successful relationship-building. Demonstrating empathy, active listening, and clear communication can differentiate you from competitors and help you establish meaningful connections with decision-makers.

Oprah Winfrey exemplifies a leader who excels in emotional intelligence and communication. Her ability to connect with audiences on a deep emotional level has been a key factor in her success as a talk show host, media executive, and philanthropist. Oprah's genuine interest in people's stories and her skillful communication have allowed her to build a vast network of influential relationships that extend beyond the media industry.

The Influence of Relationship-Building in Business

Demonstrating that you can enhance business success through relationship-building is invaluable. Companies that prioritize relationship-building are often more resilient in the face of challenges and better positioned for long-term success.

- **Warren Buffett**, the CEO of Berkshire Hathaway, is known for his people-centric approach to investing and business management. Buffett places a high value on building relationships with the companies he invests in and often stresses the importance of integrity and trust. His approach has earned him a reputation as a reliable and ethical leader, contributing to the long-term success of Berkshire Hathaway.

- **Howard Schultz's** focus on relationships and customer experience has been a critical factor in Starbucks' global expansion.

- **Richard Branson's** commitment to employee satisfaction and strong partnerships has been central to Virgin's diverse business success.

- **Oprah Winfrey's** emotional intelligence and communication prowess have been instrumental in building her media empire.

Being a great people connector is not just a desirable skill but an essential one for business success. Position yourself as a trusted advisor to your customers and as an ambassador for your company throughout the industry and beyond. Show up when it counts. Be a good partner, whether that means forging bonds with your internal teammates or your largest supplier. Ensure your communication skills and emotional intelligence are top-notch, and demonstrate to decision-makers that you have the influence to enhance their business success.

6. The Motivator

We all have those days when the thought of getting out of bed and heading to work feels like a Herculean task. You hit snooze multiple times, begrudgingly get up, and wonder how you're supposed to motivate anyone else when you can barely motivate yourself. But guess what? You shouldn't rely solely on those in leadership positions to inspire your coworkers and create a positive vibe at work.

Here's how you can make a difference and boost everyone's energy levels—even on your most sluggish days.

Hype Up Your Peers

When your brain is still booting up and that caffeine kick hasn't hit yet, focus on hyping up your colleagues. Celebrate their wins and cheer them on as if they just won a gold medal. Did someone finally crack a complex algorithm or ace a presentation? Let them know it's epic! Everyone loves having cheerleaders, and your enthusiasm will help get those positive vibes flowing.

- Send a quick shout-out in your team chat.
- Instigate high-five sessions or celebration moments.
- Be that friend who says, "You totally crushed it!"

Be the Go-To Work Friend

Work can be a rollercoaster, with its ups, downs, and unexpected challenges. Be the person your coworkers can lean on when they're stuck on a problem or need advice. Even if you don't have all the answers, being a supportive ear makes a huge difference. Sometimes, all someone needs is a friendly face and a bit of encouragement to keep going.

- Ask who needs help when you sense they're stressed.
- Offer to brainstorm ideas over coffee or an energy drink.

You Next

- Remind them, "You've got this!" when they doubt themselves.

Be Open to Conversations

Sometimes people just need someone to talk to, whether it's about work stress or that cliffhanger from last night's episode. Open up and encourage genuine conversations with your colleagues. Being approachable and relatable will help others feel comfortable and connected.

- Start by asking open-ended questions: "How's your day going?" instead of "How are you?"
- Share something relatable from your own experiences.
- Listen actively; sometimes, people just need to vent.

Celebrate the Little Wins

Big achievements are fantastic, but let's not forget about the little wins that keep the workplace moving. Celebrate these smaller victories with your colleagues to boost morale and show that every bit of progress counts.

Share Your Interests and Curiosity

When you're passionate about something, it rubs off on others. Talk about what excites you, whether it's a new project, a book you're reading, or a hobby you've picked up. Your enthusiasm can inspire your coworkers to find their own passions and engage more deeply in their work. Be genuinely curious about what excites others and ask questions.

Practice Empathy and Understanding

Everyone has off days, and showing empathy can really help. Be that colleague who offers a shoulder to lean on and genuinely cares about the well-being of others. Your understanding nature can make work feel like a safe space, even when things get hectic.

Chapter Eight: Make Yourself Invaluable

- Notice when someone seems down and check in with them.
- Be non-judgmental and offer encouragement where you can.
- Simply ask, "How can I support you today?"

Fuel Team Spirit

Remember, a motivated team is a winning team. Bring people together by fostering a sense of community and belonging. Your efforts to create a supportive and energetic work environment can drive team performance to new heights. Even if you are not in a leadership position, you can:

- Organize team lunches.
- Hold virtual coffee breaks.
- Remember birthdays.

Motivating others doesn't mean you have to be the most enthusiastic person in the room 24/7. It's about being there for your colleagues, lifting each other up, and creating a positive atmosphere where everyone can thrive. With your great attitude and commitment to positivity, you can help transform your workplace into a place where people look forward to showing up every day. Plus, you'll build a reputation as someone who's not just reliable but also inspiring—qualities that will undoubtedly help you stand out as a young professional with leadership potential.

When you capture and spread the spark of engagement needed to make your team work at higher levels, you will become known as a motivator and a worthy candidate for a higher leadership position.

7. The "Rock"

People love working with those who keep their promises and dislike working with those who don't. The takeaway? If you say you're going to do it, do it! This may sound like a simple lesson from elementary school, but you might be surprised at how rare it is in the business world.

In today's fast-paced environment, people are stretched thin with numerous projects, and things often fall through the cracks. Phone calls go unanswered, deadlines slip by, and emails linger in inboxes. While these occurrences are common, they also present an enormous opportunity for you to stand out by doing the opposite—consistently delivering on your commitments.

Position yourself as The Rock by making reliability, dependability, and consistency part of your core values. This starts with being honest about your capabilities. Don't agree to commitments you can't fulfill; be realistic about what you can take on. However, once you commit to something, ensure you follow through and do it well.

Build a reputation for being on time, showing up even when attendance isn't mandatory, pitching in to help others, and being fully present at work and during meetings. Aim to finish projects ahead of deadlines—not just some of the time, but all the time. This level of consistency will undoubtedly get you noticed and recognized.

Make yourself invaluable by leveraging your unique experiences and enthusiasm for your industry. Be intentional about how you present yourself at work and outside of the office. People will remember how you show up in all areas of your life.

In the next chapter, we'll discuss how to build a strong mental and physical foundation to support your reliability and effectiveness.

MAKE IT HAPPEN!

Identify a niche you can claim to become the employee your company can't afford to lose.

- ☐ The Expert
- ☐ The Idea Generator
- ☐ The Solution Finder
- ☐ The Efficiency Guru
- ☐ The Relationship Builder
- ☐ The Motivator
- ☐ The Rock

For more valuable tips, visit YouNextNow.com!

CHAPTER NINE

BUILD A
Solid Foundation

Bill was the director of a multi-billion-dollar manufacturing company. He knew the business like the back of his hand, possessed years of diverse experience, and was well-liked by his peers. However, when the executive team convened to discuss a potential promotion for Bill, they quickly reached a consensus.

Unfortunately for Bill, it was not good news. They decided to withdraw him from consideration.

The reason for their decision? Bill frequently allowed other aspects of his life to interfere with his focus on work. In other words, personal drama routinely encroached upon his professional space.

One of Bill's adult children struggled with addiction, often requiring medical care and law enforcement intervention. For two years, Bill used all his vacation and sick days trying to bail his son out of jail or traveling to see him at rehab centers. He also incurred a range of unanticipated financial obligations in his efforts to support his son, even taking out a second mortgage on his home. The stress and debt took a serious toll on Bill's mental health, work performance, and effectiveness as a team member.

Initially, his team members and supervisor were very supportive. They didn't mind stepping in for him at sales meetings or making client calls—at first. They understood his late arrivals, exhausted eyes, and missed deadlines—at first.

They wanted to support Bill as he struggled to help his son. But as time passed, resentment grew. Colleagues stopped counting on Bill. His son's personal drama was more than a distraction; it was the primary reason for Bill's downfall at the company.

People will support personal crises, but when there appeared to be no end to the drama, and after coworkers and his team extended as much grace as they could, they eventually grew tired of excuses and the extra workload. Bill tried to balance his family with work, but he simply couldn't. Everyone sympathized with Bill's untenable situation, but ultimately, the work needed to get done, and Bill wasn't fulfilling his responsibilities. The situation deteriorated from bad to worse.

We all have lives outside of our jobs—or at least we should. It's normal for people to occasionally miss work for illness, a child's soccer game, or a sudden lunch opportunity with friends in town. That's just part of the human experience! But in Bill's case, a new crisis every week severely distracted him from his job commitments, adding to his cumulative tension and anxiety.

The unfortunate reality was that everyone around the conference table agreed Bill could handle the responsibilities of a new job in an ideal world. They simply didn't believe he could take on additional responsibilities until he got his life in order. No successful organization can continually lower its standards to accommodate the lowest common denominator or the weakest link. At some point, a pure assessment of performance in the assigned or

Chapter Nine: Build A Solid Foundation

proposed role must occur. You might not be fired for your personal issues; however, they must factor into any consideration for promotion.

While it may seem unfair to make professional decisions based on personal issues, the two are inherently linked. Whether we sit at our desks in sharp suits or lounge on the sofa in pajamas, we remain the same person. Our professional thoughts and concerns don't have sharp boundaries that cease at 5:00 PM; we can't entirely block out personal issues during the workday.

What does this mean for you?

Consider whether your career might be stalled due to your supervisor's concerns about how you are managing your life challenges in a broader, 24/7 context. If you want to be seen as promotable, you need to take as many steps as possible to present yourself as a low-risk option.

Supervisors are judged based on whom they recommend for promotions. They can never know with 100% certainty whether someone will be able to step into a new role and perform at peak capacity. They are essentially making a bet: if you succeed, they look like heroes; if you fail, they share in the responsibility. Think about their perspective when they are deciding who advances.

Even if you perform exceptionally at work, how are things going in the rest of your life? How likely are you to encounter a personal crisis that could prevent you from reaching your next-level potential? The decision-makers regarding your career are looking for a drama-free, low-risk, high-reward individual.

What can you do, starting right now, to become a better candidate for promotion? We recommend building a solid foundation in the following areas:

1. Physical health and fitness

At the risk of sounding like your mom, we feel compelled to share the basics here: eat a balanced diet, get enough sleep, and exercise regularly. These may not be groundbreaking revelations, but they are essential for keeping your brain healthy and functioning at an optimal level.

I know it sounds like something your mom would say, but don't do drugs and expect to get promoted. I had a talented young woman, Tabitha, who worked for me. She was highly qualified and had an impressive educational background that helped her shine. The problem? She dated someone who smoked pot every day. That shouldn't have been an issue, but he convinced her to try it.

Now, yes, we know many people use medical marijuana, and yes, we know all drugs—even legal ones—can cause problems, and yes, we know we sound like your parents. But once she tried it, she was hooked, and Tabitha became the poster child for the stereotypical pot user.

She was habitually late for work.

She missed deadlines.

She lacked ambition.

She no longer took pride in her appearance.

Her addiction was evident. After repeated attempts to help her kick the habit and weeks of company-funded rehab, we had to let her go because she was not interested in changing. She simply liked being an addict.

We have countless stories of how someone's lack of control or addiction ruined their careers, relationships, and lives. Please understand our intent in sharing this: we want you to be wildly successful.

Here is some advice based on years of coaching experience, along with responses to common comments we've heard.

Chapter Nine: Build A Solid Foundation

Comment: "I can't understand why they won't promote me."

Response: "Are you saying the right things in front of clients?"

Comment: Well, I'm young. I want to have fun! I can get by on a few hours of sleep. We always go out on Thursday nights and close the club down at 2 a.m."

Response: "Everyone at work knows you are hungover and unproductive on Fridays. This is eroding trust."

Comment: "I want to get in shape, but I never seem to have time."

Response: "Are you making a consistent effort to schedule physical activity?"

Comment: "I can't understand why they won't promote me."

Response: "Do you look the part? Do you present as executive material?"

Comment: "I can roll out of bed and be at the office in seven minutes."

Response: "And it looks like you just rolled out of bed. That is not how senior executives present themselves."

You get the point, right? If you're serious about advancing your career, take your health seriously. When you are healthy and fit, you send a signal that you care about being in shape to perform your best. If two candidates for promotion have equal job performance, external factors will be considered, even if no reviewer explicitly states them.

2. Mental and spiritual health

We can't ignore this part of the equation, and neither should you.

Ask yourself some serious questions: How are you handling stress these days? Are you working to maintain an appropriate work/life balance, or are you constantly burning the candle at both ends?

Life can be tough, and it's fair to say that every day isn't going to be all rainbows and butterflies. The question is whether you know how to manage those inevitable hurdles. Do you maintain a positive attitude and confidently navigate the challenges? Or do you grab an extra-large bag of Nacho Cheese Doritos and hide in the closet? (If it's always the latter, you might want to revisit the first section about physical health. Just sayin'...)

Your mental and emotional health are critical components of professional success. If you find yourself struggling with an issue, don't hesitate to reach out for help. Contact a family member, a trusted friend, or a licensed counselor. Your company may even offer free services as part of your benefits package. There's no trophy for going it alone, so seek the support you need to show up at work in the best possible frame of mind to be productive and successful.

As for your spiritual health, that also deserves your attention. We understand that people have different belief systems, but we encourage professionals to carve out time to consider the bigger issues that impact their lives: faith, values, morals, and ethics. Where do you stand on these matters? What do you believe? How do these guiding principles influence your attitudes and behaviors at home and at work?

Whether you believe in God, a higher power, or something else, you can demonstrate your values and principles through your everyday actions: the way you treat your co-workers, the community causes you support, and the approaches you take when faced with difficult situations.

Chapter Nine: Build A Solid Foundation

When you are spiritually healthy, you feel connected to something greater than yourself and have more confidence in your life's purpose. That's the type of foundation many leaders use to create highly successful careers. Some might say their spiritual connections give them an advantage when it comes to aligning with the corporate vision. They understand how that greater purpose leads them toward a destination and makes the journey more meaningful.

3. Financial health

People who get promoted to higher levels within an organization often demonstrate their ability to manage their finances successfully. In fact, in the military, excessive personal debt can prevent someone from obtaining security clearance. If you mistreat your creditors and ignore your debt obligations, can you truly be trusted with sensitive company data? Your financial health matters.

Individuals with finances that represent a significant vulnerability may be tempted to make poor decisions on the job. Ethical lines that others wouldn't cross could become blurred if an opportunity for personal profit is involved.

This was one of the red flags for Bill. The company leaders had been very supportive of his family problems, and no one could blame him for wanting to help his son. Any of us could end up in that situation. However, for Bill, his financial complications were nonstop. He had become consumed with trying to find new ways to cover his son's treatment and legal fees.

The job Bill was being considered for involved managing a $27 million budget. The executive team simply couldn't overlook the idea that his ongoing drama and increasing debt would distract him from handling significantly greater financial responsibilities. That might not seem fair or empathetic, but the company's profitability was at stake. The executive team made a prudent choice.

You Next

If you need help figuring out your finances, check out Mary's book, Money Smart: For 18-30 Year-Olds Who Want to Live Well and Retire Comfortably. It is available on Amazon.

You can download the Money Smart workbook for free here: www.ProductiveLeaders.com/MoneySmart.

4. *Relationship health*

Successful leaders possess personal qualities that allow them to form and sustain positive relationships. To be clear, there's no requirement to have a "significant other" to advance in your career. What is necessary is evidence of strong, lasting relationships with family members and friends. Workplace challenges escalate with higher job titles, so you want to have a support system of people who will be there for you when things get tough—or to help celebrate your wins!

Keep these considerations in mind to make yourself an appealing candidate for a higher job title:

Avoid Red Flags for Decision-Makers

Decision-makers may be wary of promoting individuals whose personal lives are excessively chaotic for extended periods. This concern stems from the belief that personal instability may reflect a person's judgment and reliability. If someone cannot manage their personal relationships effectively, it raises questions about their ability to handle work relationships. For example, if an employee is constantly dealing with personal drama, it may be perceived that they could bring similar instability into the workplace.

History is full of examples of prominent individuals whose personal lives adversely affected their professional careers.

John Edwards, the former U.S. Senator and Vice-Presidential candidate, saw his promising political career derailed by revelations of an extramarital affair and a child out of wedlock, coupled with the misuse of campaign funds to cover it up. The scandal not only ended his political aspirations but also brought severe legal and financial consequences.

Similarly, Tiger Woods, one of the greatest golfers of all time, saw his career and endorsements take a significant hit after his infidelity scandal broke out in 2009. The turmoil in his personal life led to a slump in his professional performance and the loss of sponsorships, underscoring how personal issues can spill over into one's career.

In the corporate world, Mark Hurd, the former CEO of Hewlett-Packard, was forced to resign amid allegations of sexual harassment and falsification of expense reports. Although Hurd denied the allegations, the scandal was enough to tarnish his reputation and end his tenure at HP. This case highlights how personal conduct, even if not criminal, can severely impact professional standing and trust.

The Importance of Personal Relationships in Leadership

Successful leaders are not only defined by their professional skills and achievements but also by their ability to maintain and nurture positive personal relationships. This is crucial because these relationships reflect your ability to handle the complexities and pressures associated with leadership roles. A leader's personal life often mirrors their professional life; stability and maturity in personal relationships can signal readiness for greater responsibilities at work.

The Impact of Personal Life on Professional Advancement

While it is not necessary to have a significant other to succeed professionally, it is essential to demonstrate the ability to maintain strong, lasting relationships with family and friends. Higher job titles bring increased workplace challenges, and having a solid support system becomes invaluable during tough times and in celebrating successes. This support system can provide the emotional stability needed to navigate the pressures of a high-stakes role.

Why Stability and Maturity Matter

Demonstrating stability and maturity in personal relationships is crucial for leaders, as it signals their ability to handle the responsibilities that come with higher roles. Leaders are often required to manage large teams and navigate complex interpersonal dynamics. Stability in personal life can provide a foundation of trust and reliability, which is essential for effective leadership.

Leaders with stable personal lives are likely to have better mental and emotional well-being, translating into more balanced decision-making and resilience under pressure. It also fosters a positive work environment, free from unnecessary drama and distractions, enhancing overall productivity and team morale.

Demonstrating stability and maturity in any of your relationships will make a statement about your readiness to handle more responsibility, potentially leading a larger team and taking on the relational challenges of working at a level with greater visibility. The hidden message? You'll be able to do your job well without creating a soap opera for everyone around you.

MAKE IT HAPPEN!

- ➤ Keep your personal life organized to present yourself as a risk-free, drama-free candidate for promotion.
- ➤ Prioritize your physical health and fitness.
- ➤ Pay attention to your mental and emotional health, especially if stress is weighing you down.
- ➤ Dedicate time to nurture your spiritual health (whatever that may look like for you).
- ➤ Manage your personal finances effectively to avoid being perceived as someone who can't handle the responsibilities of a large corporate budget.
- ➤ Build and maintain positive personal relationships to demonstrate your stability for working with—and eventually leading—a team.

For more valuable tips, visit YouNextNow.com!

CHAPTER TEN

AVOID
The Pitfalls

Maya was thrilled when she was selected to participate in her company's specialized training program, designed to fast-track young, motivated professionals. The program introduced participants to various parts of the company. They received briefings, shadowed executives, and listened to high-level discussions. Maya loved every minute of it.

After six months, Maya was a clear standout among her peers at the publishing firm. Her credentials were impressive, and she had become the go-to expert for an emerging suite of products within the organization. Maya's future looked extremely bright.

At an industry conference, Maya chatted busily with several new acquaintances during the welcome reception. She was caught off guard when a man from a competing firm began asking detailed questions about Walter, her division's executive vice president. Due to some of his comments, Maya quickly realized he suspected a financial scandal was brewing, and it seemed likely that Walter was involved.

Maya didn't know the vice president very well. Walter had a reputation for being a bold risk-taker and occasionally bending the rules to the point of crossing questionable lines, but she had no real relationship with him. He had been one of the VPs who delivered a segment of the training program.

All of that information was processing in Maya's mind as her conversation partner continued to grill her for juicy details. Perhaps it was the shocking nature of the news while being away from the office. Maybe it was the glass of wine in her hand.

She responded with a nervous laugh: "I don't know anything about it, but that doesn't sound exactly out of character. Who knows? It could be true."

> All of the chapters in this book so far have emphasized what you need to do to move your career ahead at a faster pace. There is a flip side of that coin. Sometimes knowing what NOT to do is just as valuable.

The conversation was overheard by another member of the company, who Maya didn't know but who was a close friend of the VP. A week later, Maya was accused of confirming Walter's involvement in the scandal to a competitor and making derogatory remarks about a company leader. Her reputation was damaged, and her promising career was in serious jeopardy.

All of the chapters in this book so far have emphasized what you need to do to move your career ahead at a faster pace. There is a flip side of that coin. Sometimes knowing what NOT to do is just as valuable.

Chapter Ten: Avoid The Pitfalls

SEVEN PITFALLS TO AVOID

1. Don't badmouth anyone, ever.

"If you can't say something nice, don't say it at all." Your grandmother's sage advice holds true in the workplace: someone is always listening. Even if you preface a critical comment with a qualifier, there's no guarantee that your words won't be repeated out of context. Just ask Maya; it happens.

It simply doesn't make sense to risk your professional success by gossiping, repeating information shared in confidence, or voicing unflattering observations. Challenge yourself to find the positive in every person and situation. There's always another side to the story, so give people the benefit of the doubt. Either way, you don't want to become the person known for making negative comments. If you wouldn't want it on the front page of the paper or let your mother read it, then don't say it aloud. You can think it—just don't say it.

2. Don't forget that online posts last forever.

We love social media as much as anyone else, but use caution! Your professional reputation and career could be at risk. Before hiring or promoting you, HR representatives and their algorithms will scour your online presence for anything (and we mean ANYTHING!) that even has a whiff of controversy—words or pictures.

I was working with a client who had found the perfect candidate, completed two rounds of interviews, and was ready to extend an offer. As a last precaution, they decided to check social media. It turns out the candidate was quite politically active. There is nothing wrong with that, and the company leaders did not necessarily disagree with the candidate's views. The problem was that the company had a strict policy against discussing or sharing political or religious views with team members or clients; they wanted to ensure a safe working environment and an inclusive culture. The result? The perfect candidate was no longer perfect.

Their goal is to avoid an embarrassing headline in The New York Times at some point in the future linking a top company executive with a scandalous opinion or photo. They don't want to be the ones who dropped the ball during the screening process. The fact is, they are more likely to promote someone less talented with a squeaky-clean social media image over a more qualified candidate with questionable posts, just to avoid potential liability.

Yes, you can care passionately about your ideas and opinions, but is it wise to get involved in an ugly argument on social media with someone you don't know and risk your career? Think about it. Are you really going to change their mind about their politics, religion, or whether they hate cats? Probably not. So why waste your time and energy?

While online posts can never be completely erased, start now by deleting anything your younger, more carefree self may have hastily posted on Instagram, Facebook, LinkedIn, or other sites. Then, moving forward, if you wouldn't show a post to your mom or your minister, delete it and move on.

3. Don't let your impulsive behaviors contradict your stated goals.

Keep in mind that anyone with a smartphone is walking around with a high-definition camera and video recorder at their fingertips—and they aren't afraid to use them. Not to sound like an episode of Law & Order, but whatever you say or do in public can be captured and used against you. The bottom line? Don't assume you have privacy. Don't assume that someone isn't recording you. Don't assume that because you feel anonymous in a different city or at a different event, other people don't know who you are. Words and actions that don't align with your professional ambitions can drastically impede your career progress.

If you work in a formal environment and exhibit the highest degree of professionalism during the day, don't put yourself in a position where you have to explain a video of yourself, for example, being overserved or underdressed. That kind of embarrassment can haunt you for many years.

Let me share what seems like an innocent act. I was at lunch with a group of colleagues and our boss. Our boss has a funny habit: he puts about 12 packs of artificial sweetener into an eight-ounce glass of tea. Yes, that's right—12 packs. We all thought it was funny, so a peer took a video of our boss adding the packets and then drinking the sugary concoction. We all found it hilarious, but our boss's boss did not. He found it disgusting and unprofessional, and our boss had to attend a 12-week class on professional behavior. Our boss was rightfully furious that someone shared his personal preference for how he drank his tea during a team-building lunch. It cost him time away from the office, created more work for the team, and diminished his trust in the group.

4. Don't burn your bridges.

No matter what company you work for or what industry you've chosen, it's a small world. Why limit your career potential by damaging relationships? Whatever the situation, be kind. Everything won't always go your way, but you can always choose to be gracious. This also means eliminating nonverbal cues that can broadcast your inner feelings without ever saying a word (think eye rolls, exasperated sighs, and crossed arms).

If your definition of burning bridges only involves a heated discussion with snarky language, you might want to broaden that concept. The annoying person in the next cubicle whom you avoid like the plague could end up being the hiring manager when you interview for your dream job in five years. Use polite actions and words—there's no wiggle room.

I was once at an event where the AV technician was working hard to make the event happen. A few times, he approached me and asked if I needed alone time before going on stage, as the room was small and very crowded. Did I want him to ask people to give me some space? I told him I was thrilled that people were interested in talking and that I was delighted to spend time with them.

Looking back, I wasn't sure if he was testing me or not. A few weeks later, I found out he got engaged to the CEO of the company that brought me in. No one knew, and I was 100% sure that everything I said to him and his team was repeated back to his future spouse. Thank goodness I responded the right way!

This doesn't mean you should be a doormat for anyone who wants to walk over you. It means being professional. Don't gossip about others, don't spread rumors, and don't give co-workers a reason to disparage your professionalism. Be nice, be fair, and be a good team player.

5. Don't resist change.

Change is constant, and today, its pace is accelerating rapidly. Do people generally love the idea of change? Not really. For most, change feels uncomfortable and frustrating. However, in the business world, it's a daily reality. Companies desperately need leaders who not only embrace change but also inspire their teams to do the same. By being the one who embraces change and helping others adapt, you put yourself in the driver's seat, fully in charge of your career.

If you want to be promoted, commit to continuous learning and show that you can handle change—better yet, demonstrate that you welcome it. You eat change for breakfast! You're not afraid of new processes, technologies, or initiatives. Bring. It. On!

Chapter Ten: Avoid The Pitfalls

Think about all the words that describe people who resist change:

old-fashioned	stubborn	fearful
old-school	stagnant	unhappy
stuck	scared	status quo

Now think of words that describe people who embrace change:

forward-thinking	passionate	agile
strategic	energetic	adaptable
excited	flexible	innovative

What category of words would you prefer to describe you? Probably the second group.

Set a goal to be the person on your team who proactively gets ahead of the curve with whatever comes next. By adopting this mindset, your employer will recognize your inherent value as a leader in driving change. Those who can advocate for and lead change often find themselves at the top of the list for advancement.

6. Don't be afraid to say you don't know the answer.

Even the greatest Jeopardy champions occasionally get stumped by a question. The truth is, no one can be expected to know every fact about every subject. If you're asked something and don't have the answer, honesty is the best policy.

During your plebe year at the Naval Academy (the first year), you have a limited set of responses when someone asks a professional question. One of those responses is simply, "I'll find out." While most organizations aren't as strict as military schools, many leaders grow frustrated when they have to guide their team to find answers that should be common knowledge.

The best way to handle such situations is to say, "Great question! I don't know, but I will find out and get back to you." (Just make sure you follow up!) The worst thing you can do is fumble for an answer or make something up—this rarely ends well.

The key takeaway here is to be the one who admits when they don't know something and is willing to seek out the answer.

Curious individuals are incredibly valuable. They ask questions, research answers, and think independently. When they provide information, you can trust that it's accurate.

7. Don't be afraid to admit you made a mistake.

It's part of the human experience: no one is perfect. Even the greatest athletes have their off days. Tom Brady occasionally throws a stinker of a pass. Simone Biles doesn't stick every landing. LeBron James sometimes has a performance that's less than spectacular. You, too, are not infallible.

While you might be pouring all your energy into landing that next promotion, don't let that laser focus blind you to your humanity. Here's what you need to remember: it's OK to make a mistake. (Seriously, read that sentence again.) What's not acceptable is pretending the mistake didn't happen. Trying to cover it up is even worse.

When you are honest and transparent about your errors, you earn the respect and admiration of your colleagues. It takes a strong and confident professional to admit a misstep, but the willingness to own it—and fix it—is a hallmark of great leadership.

Everyone makes mistakes. What truly reveals your character is how you respond afterward. Do you go overboard to make amends, or do you blame someone else?

Let go of the notion that you need to be perfect. If something goes wrong, speak up. Take action to make it right. Then, move on. You have more work to do.

Chapter Ten: Avoid The Pitfalls

Years ago, I worked for a leader who made a significant mistake. He owned up to it and implemented a plan to fix it, which ultimately led to greater loyalty and engagement from his team than if he had never erred.

This issue stemmed from his bad temper. Most of the time, he was easy-going, but when stress hit, he would lose control. He was oblivious to the impact until Human Resources facilitated a 360° review, where his team could anonymously share feedback.

He was stunned by how negatively his temper affected his team. Instead of denying it or justifying his behavior, he took ownership. He reflected on the feedback, hired an executive coach, and created a plan to manage his anger.

At the next all-hands meeting, he stood up, shared the feedback, expressed his thoughts, apologized, and outlined his plan for improvement. Every quarter, he asked for more feedback and updated us on his progress. It was genuinely impressive.

Remember, everyone is human—including you. You will make mistakes, so own them, fix them, and don't repeat them. Keep moving forward.

Some of the most powerful phrases leaders can use include:

"I'm sorry."

"I made a decision, and that decision was wrong, so we are going to change."

"I want to fix this."

See Appendix I for the list of Effective Phrases for Leaders.

Navigating the challenging aspects of leadership requires a clear mind and the ability to stay calm under pressure. Apply the skills you learn in your personal life to maintain strong relationships in your professional life as well.

MAKE IT HAPPEN!

- ➤ Supplement your career action plan with a clear understanding of what actions to avoid.
- ➤ Challenge yourself to find the positive in every person and situation.
- ➤ Be highly selective with anything you post on social media.
- ➤ Make sure that your public actions align with your professional goals.
- ➤ Handle difficult situations graciously to avoid damaging relationships.
- ➤ Embrace change and inspire others to do the same.
- ➤ Showcase your integrity by admitting when you don't know the answer or when you make a mistake.

For more valuable tips, visit YouNextNow.com!

CHAPTER ELEVEN

GET Noticed

When Lucas was offered a promotion to become the junior manager of a large hotel, he was genuinely shocked. His supervisor was moving into a different role and needed to fill her position. She recognized Lucas's immense potential and rewarded him with this unexpected opportunity.

Lucas was as thrilled as he was surprised, but he also felt awkward about leading his former peers. He didn't want to alienate his friends or make them feel inferior. As a result, Lucas often downplayed his leadership role and consistently shined the spotlight on his team members.

When a colleague congratulated him on a successful project, Lucas humbly shifted the credit to one of his staff members, whether they were present to hear it or not, even when he was the one responsible for the success. It seemed generous and professional to him.

He also excelled at trusting his team to do their jobs. He didn't micromanage his former peers, and while they appreciated his hands-off approach, it sometimes meant he wasn't aware of problems until his boss informed him. His boss believed Lucas when he said his teams did all the work.

Three years later, as Lucas explored opportunities to apply for a more senior position, he discovered that some people at the executive level were unaware of his competencies, including the fact that he was the youngest person to hold the position and that his teams genuinely enjoyed working for him. In his efforts to let his team take all the credit and avoid micromanaging, he had become perceived as a weak leader. To upper management, he had become almost invisible and virtually unneeded.

> To advocate for yourself when the time is right, you need to maintain a list of specific accomplishments, initiatives, and outcomes. If you don't know what you did right, how can anyone else know?

This situation often arises when individuals are promoted to lead their former peers and friends. It's a delicate balance to demonstrate your leadership skills while also showcasing the abilities of your team members.

As a leader, it's essential to shine the light on those who work for you and give credit where credit is due. However, if your boss isn't aware of your capabilities, you cannot be promoted. If your boss doesn't actively advocate for you, you must advocate for yourself.

Mary here! This was one of the toughest lessons I learned after leaving the Navy. In the Navy, it's your responsibility to get your people promoted. You train them, give them increasing levels of responsibility, and push hard for their advancement. Advocating for

Chapter Eleven: Get Noticed

your team is literally part of your job. Likewise, it's your boss's responsibility to advocate for you. But when that doesn't happen, you must advocate for yourself; otherwise, your career becomes subject to the whims of others who may not have your best interests at heart.

To advocate for yourself when the time is right, you need to maintain a list of specific accomplishments, initiatives, and outcomes. If you don't know what you did right, how can anyone else know?

It's perfectly okay to accept compliments when you deserve them. You can be modest while still owning your achievements.

Consider the responses of quarterbacks when they're interviewed after an important game. They're often asked about a specific play or pass, and their typical response is, "I am so grateful to be part of such a great team, and everyone played really hard today." What's clear is that this response also implies that the quarterback played hard, too!

Even if you're not yet in a leadership position, you still need to navigate your role as a team member aspiring for a C-suite position.

Here are the issues: Should you start hogging all the credit for team wins? Definitely not. Should you refuse to take credit for your contributions? Again, no.

Somewhere in between lies the right balance, and you need to find it. Your goal? Discover strategic ways to get noticed and build your reputation as someone destined for the executive suite while remaining humble and modest and giving credit where it is due.

Early in my career, I worked for a leader who was a master at this. We were part of a large multinational corporation, and getting noticed in a sea of 2,200 employees was not easy. Luckily for me, my boss had mastered the art.

He quickly learned what was most important to the C-suite leaders and understood what they wanted our team to accomplish.

With each level of progress we made, he ensured that the C-suite was informed, delicately striking a balance between sharing how he kept the team focused and turning the praise back to us for making it happen.

Some people labeled him as political, as if it were a negative term, but I thought he was one of the best leaders I had ever worked for. He understood—and so did I—that the stronger his reputation, the easier it was for him to shine a light on all of us.

As a result, within five years, he not only was promoted to the C-suite, but every single one of his direct reports, including me, moved into senior-level leadership positions.

As a leader, you need to attract the right attention to yourself, your team, and your division. If you want to attract positive attention as someone worthy of a promotion, you need to make that happen.

HERE ARE SIX STRATEGIES TO HELP YOU GET NOTICED:

1. Bond with your boss

We've mentioned this before, but it's worth reiterating: your immediate supervisor has the potential to be your greatest advocate. They can spread the word to upper management about your talents and contributions. The darker side of this relationship? Your boss could also be the one blocking your progress.

Without a doubt, this is a relationship you absolutely need to nurture and grow. Consistently make the effort to build and strengthen that bond. Schedule regular meetings to ensure you have adequate, uninterrupted one-on-one time to discuss your ideas, progress, and feedback, as well as find ways to increase your value to the organization.

No, that doesn't mean you should show up every morning with her favorite Starbucks beverage or take over watering her plants.

Chapter Eleven: Get Noticed

Smart leaders can spot manipulative, obsequious behavior from a mile away. Your goal is to develop a genuine relationship based on an authentic connection that grows naturally over time. Commit to investing in your boss's success, and she will help you reach your goals.

Show an interest in her life and hobbies, and find common ground. Above all, be friendly, courteous, reliable, and thoughtful. Can you volunteer to help with a task that might lighten her load? If you have the capacity to assist, do it! Always be solution-oriented. You want to be the person they think of first when a new opportunity arises.

In the context of that relationship, be open about your career goals and the path you're interested in following to advance within the company. Ask for candid feedback, support, suggestions, and advice. View your boss as a collaborative partner in achieving your objectives along the path of career progress.

2. Take on more responsibilities

While it's critical to perform your job well if you want to get promoted, you also don't want to become trapped by a limited job description. A great way to demonstrate your readiness for advancement is by taking on additional responsibilities. Request a special assignment, propose your own initiative, or ask to participate in a new committee.

If you want extra bonus points, volunteer for a challenging project that no one else wants to tackle. Most bosses appreciate risk-takers, so this move will classify you as dedicated and responsive.

That said, don't rush out to volunteer for anything and everything. During this time, you'll want to be highly selective.

When you decide to take on an extra project, think carefully about the criteria. Most importantly, choose one with the potential to add noticeable value for the company. Select something that will help expand your skill set beyond your daily role and allow you to grow in a different area. Exposure to top decision-makers or leaders in other lines of business would be an added bonus.

Whatever you choose, focus on achieving results rather than merely looking busy.

When you can demonstrate to your supervisor that you excel in versatile, multi-faceted roles, you'll be seen as someone capable of handling the complex challenges associated with higher-level positions.

3. Audition for the part you want

Those who determine whether you get promoted must ask themselves a basic question: Can we see this person succeeding at the next level? Your job is to ensure they can visualize that in vivid colors with a 3D cinematic experience that would make Steven Spielberg proud.

Every day you show up for work, you are auditioning for the role you want. Make it convincing!

Consider the characteristics you'll need after your promotion and find ways to demonstrate those in your current role. This might involve enhancing your communication skills—whether in person, by phone, or online. Show that you support your peers and can even mentor them when appropriate. Carry yourself with a level of poise and executive presence that convinces others you are leadership material right now.

Additionally, ensure you demonstrate your commitment to the organization and put in the effort to go above and beyond. Be reliable. Show up early. Meet your deadlines. Pay attention to your contributions in team meetings and presentations to showcase your leadership potential.

Chapter Eleven: Get Noticed

If you consistently exhibit these traits, your boss won't hesitate when the question arises: Do you look like someone who could succeed at the next level? Absolutely, positively, without a doubt!

4. Increase your visibility

There's more to getting noticed than simply expanding the sheer volume of names in your Outlook Address Book. As you advance within an organization, you'll need to enhance your visibility with senior decision-makers and influential individuals. This involves strategically building rapport with select contacts within your company, industry, community, and beyond. (If you lightly skimmed over Chapter Seven about networking, this might be a good time to revisit it!)

How can you increase your visibility with the people who hold the power to secure a place for you at the top? Perhaps you hear about an upcoming conference featuring a panel discussion with some of the industry's top trailblazers. Even if your company won't cover the expenses, consider investing your time and money to attend. Engage by asking thoughtful questions and be sure to introduce yourself.

What about volunteering to support one of the CEO's favorite charities? Could you start an office book club? Is there a gym near the office where many company managers work out? Think of appropriate, targeted ways to connect with the right people and become a more visible presence.

5. Think of yourself as an unofficial company ambassador

We know what you're probably thinking: "I'm not the CEO. I'm not in PR. I'm not in Sales. That's not really my job." We challenge you to take on that role anyway. It may sound odd, but stay with us.

Imagine you're attending a reception for local business professionals. Some people view these events as purely social gatherings—an open bar and an opportunity to complain about their jobs, bosses, or companies. Don't get sucked into the wining-and-whining vortex!

Regardless of your title, you represent your company when you are out in the world. This is particularly true if you're at an event with a fancy name tag displaying the company name for all to see!

If you can mentally assume an ambassadorial role, you'll instantly elevate your words and actions. You'll consistently project a positive, professional attitude that stands out. You'll likely filter your comments to ensure what you say is helpful and adds value. Plus, you'll have a strong incentive to avoid any behavior that might detract from your ambassador-like image.

One outstanding way to demonstrate this role is to be a people connector. Be proactive about linking people to your fellow co-workers. Act as a dedicated member of the organization.

"I need to introduce you to Blake in our production department. He knows a lot about that area, and I'm sure he would love to talk to you."

"Have you ever met Sienna from our HR team? She would be a great resource for you."

"Our company just helped a customer with that same problem, and they have been thrilled with the results. Could I have one of our salespeople follow up with you?"

Pay close attention to the last example. It doesn't matter whether you work in engineering or purchasing. If you find creative ways to generate business leads or attract new customers, you'll become an irreplaceable asset for your company. It's even more impressive if you're not in the Sales department.

What's the point of all this? By thinking of yourself as an unofficial company ambassador, you'll become recognized as someone who has the organization's best interests at heart. Even better, the subtle changes in behavior you adopt will cumulatively position you as an obvious choice for a promotion.

6. Gather the evidence

We saved the most important step for last. As you embark on your journey to expand your development and get noticed, be diligent about gathering proof of your value and success. Begin building your case for advancement, emphasizing components that matter from the company's perspective.

When compiling your evidence for promotability, be sure to quantify your results using numbers, percentages, and statistics:

- Signed seven new customers this quarter
- Beat the deadline by 36 hours
- Increased customer satisfaction by 21%
- Reduced expenses by $93,000

Impressive, right? However, all the accomplishments in the world won't make a difference in your career if your boss isn't aware of them.

Don't wait to share the news until your annual performance review, a quarterly assessment, or when you formally ask for a promotion. Today's victory might be old news by then. This underscores why regular meetings with your supervisor are so important. Take advantage of those appointments to share your success stories.

Ideally, you should strive to create a constant stream of communication with your supervisor that demonstrates you are worthy of moving up in the organization. If a customer sends a letter raving about your work, ensure your boss gets a copy. Forward the email from the Senior VP who praised your contributions to the last project. Were you nominated for an award? Don't keep that a secret.

You Next

Don't just receive praise; send it too! If someone does a good job and works in another company or department, ask them for their boss's email address so you can pass on the compliment. When you send the brief email to their boss, BCC the employee as well. Consider BCCing your own boss too. Expect these results:

- The employee will gladly offer you greater help in the future.
- Their boss will be impressed that you were thoughtful enough to send the compliment.
- Their boss will think, "That company (or that department) is really squared away!"

Don't be surprised if their boss calls your boss to compliment YOU!

The people making crucial decisions about your career won't know the full scope of your capabilities if you don't take responsibility for sharing that information. Help them stay informed and steadily build your case for moving up.

We hope you gained a deeper understanding from this chapter about the importance of promoting yourself and your team as a leader. Far too often, leaders master one or the other—they heavily promote themselves or solely their team members. To excel as a leader, you need to do both.

MAKE IT HAPPEN!

- Be strategic about highlighting your career success and potential so you are noticed by key decision-makers.
- Develop an excellent relationship with your boss and clearly express your interest in advancement.
- Take on additional responsibilities and assignments with the greatest possibility of impact at the corporate level.
- Show up every day looking, acting, and sounding like a leader so that decision-makers can easily see you working at a higher level.
- Selectively increase your visibility with senior leaders so they know who you are and the contributions you have made.
- Elevate your image by thinking of yourself as an unofficial company ambassador and allowing that "filter" to positively influence your words and actions.
- Regularly share with your boss the quantifiable proof of value you have added to the company.

For more valuable tips, visit YouNextNow.com!

CHAPTER TWELVE

MAKE
Your Move

David was doing all the right things to position himself for a promotion at his advertising agency. He had been diligent about his professional development, maintained a great relationship with his boss, and worked closely with a mentor. David was a textbook example of how to get noticed and prove his value to the company.

But unfortunately for David, he had been procrastinating on the final step of the process.

Which step was David procrastinating? He had done the work to prove his value, but if he wanted to secure this promotion, he needed to formally ask for it. Now was the time to take control of his career. This would be the ultimate take-charge act. He had worked hard, covered every step, and documented his successes. So why was he hesitating?

David isn't alone; many high-potential individuals get cold feet about directly asking for a better title and more money. Some believe, perhaps due to their upbringing, that supervisors should be experienced enough to recognize and promote talent. Others think that strong hints will nudge their supervisors toward advocating for a job upgrade. (Spoiler alert: they won't!)

Don't rely on others to manage your career and life. Schedule an appointment and boldly ask for what you want and deserve (if you've done the work). No, it isn't easy or comfortable. It may feel presumptuous or overeager. It can even be downright intimidating.

We understand—that's why we developed this guide to help you through the process. Before you dive in, let me share my story about why asking for a promotion is so crucial.

Like many young professionals, I fell for the belief that if I worked hard enough, someone would notice. All I needed to do was perform well in my role, and eventually, someone would tap me on the shoulder for a promotion. When that didn't happen, I mistakenly thought, "I just need to work harder. If I put in a little more effort, my boss and the leaders of this organization will notice and promote me."

Guess what? That never happened. No one seemed to recognize how hard I was working. If anyone did know, they didn't discuss my future or any increased responsibilities with me. This situation made me frustrated. Instead of taking proactive steps, I wallowed in self-pity and endlessly complained to my girlfriends. Did I talk to my boss? Nope! I just vented to friends.

And I must have complained a lot, because they eventually grew tired of hearing it. My friends encouraged me to be direct and ask my boss for the promotion.

"You're already miserable. What harm can it do to ask?"

At first, I was indignant. I shouldn't have to ask; I had worked hard and deserved it. Good points, right? But one friend, the ringleader, challenged me: did I want to be right, or did I want to get promoted? That pushed me to my limit.

Chapter Thirteen: Engage High-Potential Talent

The night before my meeting, just before I lost my nerve, I emailed my boss to request a meeting. To my surprise, he replied immediately, asking me to come to his office at 7:30 a.m. I admit, I almost backed out. I was a little scared about what I had just done.

But the next morning, I found the courage to talk to my boss. I explained that I envisioned a future for myself at the company and wanted to advance. I shared that I believed I was doing all the right things but needed to know what else I could do and what he needed from me to promote me.

Whew! I felt proud of myself for finding my voice. But then came the dead silence. My boss didn't say anything for what felt like an hour—though it was probably only thirty seconds. Finally, he looked me straight in the eye and said, "Meridith, you are my best employee. I count on you for everything, and I see a bright future for you here." He continued, "I'm so sorry. We've been busy, and I've forgotten to tell you that you're doing great. Even though I should have said something sooner, you shouldn't have waited so long to speak up for yourself."

It was a huge lesson for me. When you do the work and perform well, you must also let leaders know you're ready to advance.

If you want something, find your courage and your voice, and ask for it.

Now on to the Checklist

One way to boost your confidence before that conversation is to complete this checklist. It's a great way to think through all the logistics of your request, identify potential objections, and prepare to counter any obstacles. We cannot emphasize enough: preparation is key! Don't make this an impulsive action or let emotions take over. You are asking for a promotion because you already bring great value to the organization, and you want to contribute even more.

THE CHECKLIST: ASK FOR A PROMOTION

1. Assess Your Developmental Readiness

- Skills & Talents: Do you possess the necessary skills and talents for a higher position?
- Education & Certifications: Have you obtained the required education and certifications?
- Experience: Do you have the relevant experience needed for the role?
- Commitment: Have you clearly communicated your commitment to the organization and your desire to advance to your supervisor?
- Feedback: Have you sought constructive feedback and implemented improvements based on that feedback?

2. Understand the Promotion Process

- Decision-Makers: Do you know exactly who is involved in the promotion decision?
- Criteria: Have you consistently performed at a superior level that justifies asking for a promotion?
- Documentation: Have you documented and quantified your successes?
- Visibility: Are the decision-makers aware of your achievements?
- Competition: Who are you competing against for this promotion (internal or external candidates)?
- Personnel Changes: What personnel changes need to occur for the new position to become available?
- Preparation: Have you reviewed your request and presentation with a mentor or colleague before officially asking for the promotion?

3. Demonstrate Leadership and Planning

- **Leadership Skills:** Have you showcased your ability to lead teams and motivate colleagues?
- **Role Research:** Can you demonstrate that you have thoroughly researched the new role and its responsibilities?
- **Case for Promotion:** Have you prepared a factual case for your promotion, including a concise summary of your accomplishments (1-2 pages)?
- **Value Addition:** Can you articulate how your achievements have specifically added value to the company?
- **Mentorship:** Have you shadowed or been mentored by someone in the desired position?
- **Training Your Replacement:** Are you actively training someone to take over your current responsibilities?
- **90-Day Plan:** Have you crafted a plan outlining what you would do during your first 90 days in the new role?

4. Be Savvy About Timing

- **Timing:** Is now the right time to ask for a promotion?
- **Situational Awareness:** Are there any ongoing situations that could negatively impact your chances (e.g., recent layoffs, loss of a big contract, personal emergencies)?
- **Recognition:** Would it be beneficial to ask for the promotion after being recognized for a successful project or receiving an award?

5. Identify Your Goals for Advancement

- **Power:** Are you seeking more power?
- **Prestige:** Do you want more prestige?
- **Influence:** Is your goal to have more influence?
- **Responsibility:** Are you looking for more responsibility?
- **Compensation:** Do you desire more money?
- **Benefits:** Are enhanced benefits a priority for you?

- Other: What else do you hope to gain from this advancement?

6. Determine Your Desired Impact

- People Development: Do you want to develop your team members?
- Results: Is increasing results a primary goal?
- Strategic Direction: Are you aiming to set a strategic direction?
- Leadership Depth: Do you want to advance the depth of leadership within the organization?
- Personal Growth: Are you focused on growing as a leader and influencer?
- Organizational Transformation: Is transforming the organization a key goal for you?
- Other: What other impacts do you wish to make on your team and the organization?

See Appendix J for a fillable checklist.

After working through the checklist, you'll have a precise outline for how to approach the final step in your promotion process:

- Where to Go: Identify the right department or individual within the company based on your qualifications.
- Who to Ask: Determine the appropriate person to request the promotion from.
- What to Say: Prepare your case to demonstrate your value effectively.
- When to Ask: Choose the optimal timing for your request.
- Why You Want to Move Up: Clearly articulate your motivations for seeking advancement.

Chapter Thirteen: Engage High-Potential Talent

These components will shape the scope of your conversation about taking on more responsibility. The good news? If you've consistently applied the strategies discussed in previous chapters, your promotion request will feel like a natural next step, not a surprise.

Use phrases such as, "I want to take the next logical step" and "with our growth in my area of expertise, I can assume more work."

Present your evidence of success confidently, be specific about your desires, and directly ask for the promotion. This crucial step empowers you to take charge of your career and future.

Weighing Your Options

Let's discuss the potential outcomes of your promotion request.

If you communicate professionally and support your case with evidence of your accomplishments, you'll likely impress your boss. However, while we can't guarantee a promotion (if we could, we'd charge a lot more for this book!), we can outline possible scenarios.

Best-Case Scenario: You present compelling evidence demonstrating your worth, and all decision-makers agree to grant your request. You'll soon find yourself packing up your current office and making dinner reservations at that trendy sushi spot to celebrate!

Worst-Case Scenario: You don't receive the response you were hoping for. Before you consider a drastic career change—like singing for tips in the subway—take a moment to reframe the situation.

Sometimes, external factors are beyond your control. Perhaps there isn't a position available at the moment, or the company simply can't offer a financial reward right now. While this can be disappointing, remember the positive outcomes of having this crucial conversation:

- **Visibility:** You've positioned yourself prominently before company leaders as someone eager for advancement.

- **Quantified Value:** By articulating your achievements, you may prompt decision-makers to seek opportunities for you rather than risk losing you to another company.

- **Negotiation Potential:** You could negotiate for additional perks or a bonus.

- **Future Timeline:** You might establish a timeline for a potential promotion down the line.

These outcomes are significant! Not every effort leads directly to a promotion, but all is not lost. Keep in mind that many successful leaders faced setbacks along their career paths.

Remember playing the board game Candyland? Sometimes you have to take a few steps back or, gasp, return to the beginning. But just when you think you've lost your momentum, a shortcut appears that puts you back on track. Career progression is rarely a straight line; don't let a bump in the road discourage you. You're still in control!

Evaluating Your Next Steps

In many ways, the ball is now in your court. You've invested considerable time and effort into making yourself highly marketable and demonstrating your value. If your current company lacks the opportunities you seek in a reasonable timeframe, you have solid credentials to explore other job options.

Take some time to weigh your options and consider the short-term and long-term implications of staying versus moving on. Reflect on the following questions to gain perspective:

- **Response Type:** Did you receive a firm "no," or was it more of a "not yet"?

- **Reconsideration Timeline:** Were they open to revisiting your request within an acceptable timeframe?

Chapter Thirteen: Engage High-Potential Talent

- Other Concessions: Did they offer any other benefits in the interim?
- Future Opportunities: Do you see growth potential with this company?
- Advantages of Staying: Are there compelling reasons to remain (e.g., brand prestige, convenient commute, superior benefits)?
- Alternative Companies: What other companies might align better with your career goals?
- Relocation Considerations: Would changing jobs require relocation or lifestyle adjustments?
- Market Research: Have you researched potential salaries, benefits packages, employee satisfaction levels, and turnover rates to make informed comparisons with your current position?

Deciding whether to stay or go is never easy, but you've positioned yourself well with your current or potential employers. After all your hard work, the choice is yours. Evaluate both options carefully, considering their short-term and long-term implications for your career.

- Do you see potential for growth within the company?
- Are there advantages to staying, such as brand prestige, commute convenience, or superior benefits?
- What other companies might be a better fit, and what changes would a move entail?
- Have you researched salaries, benefits, satisfaction, and turnover rates to make a fair comparison?

You Next

Your Career: Take Control of What Comes Next!

1. **Define your direction.**
   Get clarity on your skills, purpose and career vision.

2. **Develop your plan.**
   Create a specific strategy to achieve your goals.

3. **Get instant impact.**
   Make immediate changes to upgrade your reputation.

4. **Elevate your leadership skills.**
   Enhance your emotional intelligence to demonstrate your value.

5. **Be a team player.**
   Show your true potential by leveraging the group dynamic.

6. **Expand your network.**
   Target your connections to maximize your opportunities.

7. **Make yourself invaluable.**
   Set yourself apart from your peers in a meaningful way.

8. **Build a solid foundation.**
   Maintain good health to reduce your promotability risk.

9. **Avoid the pitfalls.**
   Increase your career marketability by knowing what NOT to do.

10. **Get noticed.**
    Prepare a solid case for your advancement.

11. **Make your move.**

    Ask for the promotion.

This decision is challenging, but your efforts have positioned you favorably with your current or a new company.

MAKE IT HAPPEN!

- ➢ Complete the Ask for a Promotion Checklist to ensure you are fully prepared.
- ➢ Make sure you understand the proper procedures to use for advancement.
- ➢ Be smart about the timing of your request.
- ➢ Present your evidence and ask for the promotion.
- ➢ Move up and celebrate—or analyze the response to determine the best option for your career.

For more valuable tips, visit YouNextNow.com!

CHAPTER THIRTEEN

ENGAGE
High-Potential Talent

We surveyed high-potential young employees to understand what motivates them at work, the skills they consider essential for future success, and how senior leaders can better support their professional development. The insights provided aim to help organizations retain top talent and effectively prepare these employees for leadership roles.

Key Findings

- High-potential employees are motivated by opportunities for learning, making a difference, and gaining greater autonomy in their roles.
- Essential skills for future positions include strategic thinking, leadership, and effective communication.

You Next

- Leadership support is crucial for providing career development plans, mentorship, and opportunities for practical experience on the job.

As the workforce rapidly evolves, understanding what motivates high-potential employees and what they need to succeed becomes increasingly important for organizations. These employees represent the future leaders of the company, and their retention and development are critical for long-term success.

Survey Methodology

The survey was completed by 86 high-potential young employees, achieving a 95% completion rate. Respondents represented a variety of industries and held different roles, providing a diverse perspective on their motivations and needs for success.

The survey focused on several key areas:

- Motivation for seeking increased responsibility
- Skills needed for future roles
- Development opportunities available in their organizations
- Obstacles to achieving professional goals
- Factors influencing their loyalty and desire to stay with their current company.

Key Findings

Motivation for Increased Responsibility

The survey revealed that 42% of high-potential employees are highly motivated (rated 5 on a scale of 1 to 5) to advance into positions of greater authority and responsibility. The top motivators for this ambition include:

Chapter Thirteen: Engage High-Potential Talent

- Making a difference (79%)
- Learning new skills and competencies (63%)
- Gaining experience (64%)
- Higher compensation (63%)

Graph 1: Motivations for Increased Responsibility

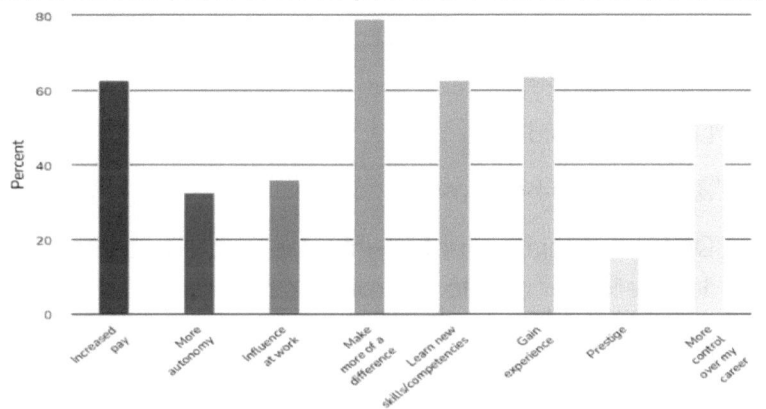

Value	Percent	Responses
Increased pay	62.8%	54
More autonomy	32.6%	28
Influence at work	36.0%	31
Make more of a difference	79.1%	68
Learn new skills/competencies	62.8%	54
Gain experience	64.0%	55
Prestige	15.1%	13
More control over my career	51.2%	44

Making bold decisions and trusting your instincts can profoundly shape the course of your life. Many individual respondents from the survey reflected on the importance of acting decisively, even when faced with uncertainty.

They were prompted to give advice to their younger selves, and their responses are as follows:

"You were right about taking that gap year; you would have lost the scholarship either way."

"Stay away from bad relationships, and buy that condo yesterday."

"Don't go into something just because you think it fits what everyone else wants you to do. Love authentically and live a life you love every single day."

"Don't be afraid to take risks."

"Be brave and bold; you've got this."

"Don't be afraid to ask for what you want. Don't limit yourself, and don't let other people control your destination."

"Do it sooner."

"Invest in the market."

This advice underscores the importance of making decisions that align with your personal values and long-term happiness.

2. Skills Needed for Future Roles

When asked about the skills they believe are necessary for their future positions, respondents highlighted the following:

- Strategic Thinking (84%)
- Leadership (78%)
- Communication (76%)
- Problem-Solving (63%)

Chapter Thirteen: Engage High-Potential Talent

These results indicate a strong desire among high-potential employees to develop skills that are critical for leadership roles.

Graph 2: Essential Skills for Future Roles

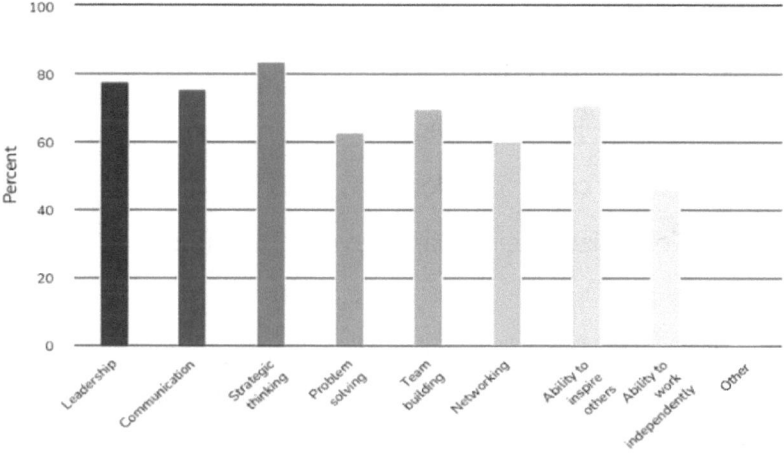

Skills Needed for Future Roles

Value	Percent	Responses
Leadership	77.9%	67
Communication	75.6%	65
Strategic thinking	83.7%	72
Problem solving	62.8%	54
Team building	69.8%	60
Networking	60.5%	52
Ability to inspire others	70.9%	61
Ability to work independently	46.5%	40
Other - if other please list in the option below	18.6%	16

3. Development Opportunities and Leadership Support

The survey also explored how current leadership can assist high-potential employees in achieving their professional goals. The top forms of support identified were:

- Mentorship (76%)
- On-the-job experience (65%)
- Formal career development plans (48%)
- Formalized training and development (52%)

High-potential employees value both structured and informal opportunities for growth, and they look to their leaders for guidance and support. Survey respondents advised their younger selves to take risks, as taking risks is often necessary for both personal and professional development. Many individuals emphasized the importance of stepping out of their comfort zones and seizing opportunities.

"Don't be afraid to take risks."

"Learn a trade. Network. Get into housing early."

"Don't be afraid to pursue certain opportunities—like playing for that team you were too nervous to join or making better decisions regarding peer pressure, especially in sports."

"Chase your dreams; don't settle for what worked for prior generations. Work for yourself."

Taking risks can lead to significant growth and unexpected opportunities.

Chapter Thirteen: Engage High-Potential Talent

Graph 3: Development Opportunities and Leadership Support

How can your current leadership help you achieve your professional goals?

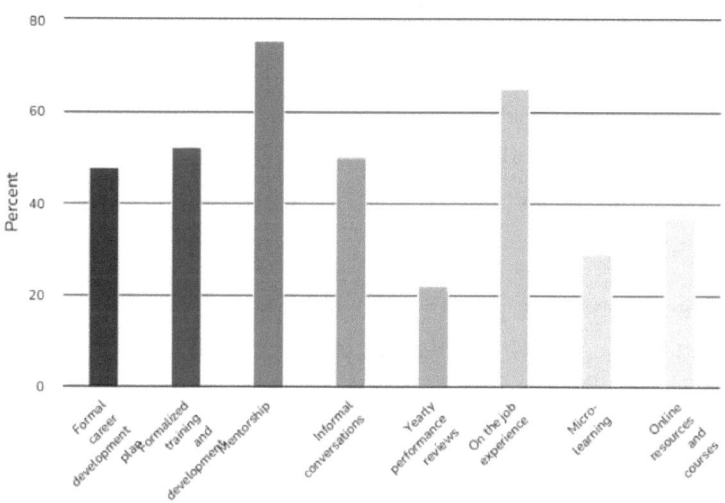

Value	Percent	Responses
Formal career development plan	47.7%	41
Formalized training and development	52.3%	45
Mentorship	75.6%	65
Informal conversations	50.0%	43
Yearly performance reviews	22.1%	19
On the job experience	65.1%	56
Micro-learning	29.1%	25
Online resources and courses	37.2%	32

4. Obstacles to Professional Growth

The biggest obstacles cited by respondents include:

- Lack of time to focus on professional development due to existing responsibilities.
- Need for leadership support to navigate their career paths effectively.
- Uncertainty about how to start when it comes to advancing in their careers.

These findings suggest that senior leaders need to create more time and space for their high-potential employees to concentrate on their growth.

High-potential employees must remain authentic and true to themselves if they want to experience professional growth. Being true to yourself and embracing your uniqueness is vital for a fulfilling life. Conforming to others' expectations can lead to a loss of self—something many people wish they had understood earlier.

"Just be yourself. Things will hurt, but you'll make it. Never feel the need to be anything other than yourself to be liked by others."

"You're ADHD and autistic; stop trying to be what other people want you to be, and never work for anyone other than yourself."

"Don't be so transparent to everyone around you; you're allowed to stand out!"

"Love yourself. Ignore everyone else from high school. Also, don't date that South Carolina boy for three years."

"Stop worrying about what everyone thinks, and stop envying others' success. Just focus on you and where you want to be, and create a plan to get there."

"Don't seek your self-worth in others."

Chapter Thirteen: Engage High-Potential Talent

Embracing your true self—flaws and all—leads to a life of authenticity and genuine satisfaction. Senior leaders can support their high-potential employees by providing flexibility in their roles.

5. Factors Influencing Loyalty and Retention

To increase their loyalty and desire to stay with their current company, high-potential employees identified the following factors as most important:

- Work-life balance (74%)
- Happy workplace environment (67%)
- Promotional opportunities (56%)
- Better pay (66%)

These results indicate that, beyond financial incentives, work-life balance and a positive work environment are crucial for retaining top talent.

Graph 5: Factors Influencing Loyalty and Retention

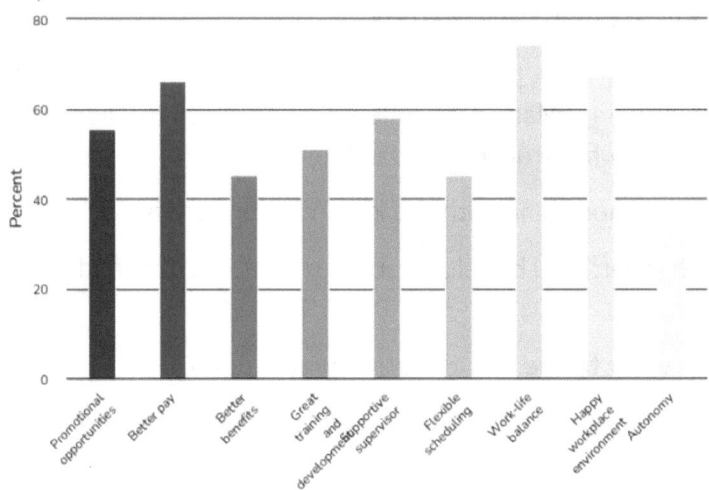

Value	Percent	Responses
Promotional opportunities	55.8%	48
Better pay	66.3%	57
Better benefits	45.3%	39
Great training and development	51.2%	44
Supportive supervisor	58.1%	50
Flexible scheduling	45.3%	39
Work-life balance	74.4%	64
Happy workplace environment	67.4%	58
Autonomy	34.9%	30

Seven Pieces of Advice to the High-Potential Employee's Younger Self

1. Prioritize What Truly Matters

Balancing work, personal life, and self-care is essential for long-term well-being. Many respondents emphasized the importance of focusing on what truly matters in life.

"Spend more time with the kids. Vacation more."

"Work hard and be reliable, but go home on time and enjoy your family."

You work to live, not the other way around."

"Value personal time—appreciate an afternoon with nothing to do."

"Prioritize! I used to give my family 'the rest of me' rather than 'the best of me.' Never want to be there again!"

"Take time to relax and enjoy the moments as they happen."

"Focus on your fitness and daily habits."

Prioritizing family, well-being, and moments of relaxation can lead to a more fulfilling and balanced life.

2. Embrace Continuous Learning

Continuous learning is vital for both personal and professional success. A recurring theme among respondents was the advice to never stop learning.

"Get higher education sooner. Show more patience with others. Set better goals, track better."

"Don't stop learning."

"Continuous learning mindset! Be alert to the changes around you and far from you. Focus on one thing at a time."

"Seek guidance from a mentor who has experience and can guide you."

"You don't know it all!"

"Take a professional course and learn local languages."

"Work harder. Get a Ph.D. Don't leave unresolved problems if you do nothing."

"Don't wait to get your master's. Do it while you're still in the school mood."

Investing in education and personal development pays dividends throughout life.

3. Establish Boundaries and Know Your Worth

Recognizing your worth and setting clear boundaries are essential for sustaining a healthy work-life balance and personal well-being. Many respondents highlighted the importance of mastering this early.

"Set boundaries—work does not define you."

"Establish firm boundaries. Set clear expectations. Know when to move on."

"Stop trying to please everyone by always saying yes to things that benefit others but not necessarily yourself."

"Do not let workplace bullies push you around. Stand up for yourself! You've earned a spot at the table and are VALUABLE, even if some don't see that. They don't determine your worth."

"Express what you think. Leave any company where you don't feel good."

"If the workplace environment is toxic, leave as soon as you can. Do not let what others think about you ruin your day."

Setting boundaries and knowing your worth are crucial for protecting your time, energy, and self-esteem.

4. Build Strong Relationships

Nurturing personal and professional relationships is crucial for a fulfilling life. Many respondents reflected on the importance of investing time and energy into building and maintaining strong connections.

"Invest time in nurturing relationships with family because I've lost some loved ones, and I only wish I had more time with them."

"Develop friendships and don't limit yourself to certain social groups. Put yourself out there!"

"Don't ever let anyone silence your voice. It is powerful and good and needs to be heard."

"Be humble and listen."

"Take time to relax and enjoy the moments as they happen."

"Work for a company that aligns with your core values. Give your best, and take the time it takes."

Strong relationships provide support, joy, and opportunities throughout life.

5. Believe in Yourself

Self-confidence is critical for overcoming challenges and achieving success. Many respondents wished they had believed in themselves sooner and not let doubt hold them back.

"Believe in yourself and your abilities, and don't let people tear you down."

"Stop worrying about what everyone thinks. And stop envying others' success. Focus on you and where you want to be, and create a plan to get there."

"You are stronger and more knowledgeable than you were led to believe.

You can make a difference in people's lives."

"Focus on the positive and don't let others define your potential."

"You can do anything you set your mind to!"

Believing in your worth and potential is key to pursuing your goals and overcoming obstacles.

6. Enjoy the Journey

Life is about the journey, not merely the destination. Many respondents encouraged their younger selves to savor life more and not take everything too seriously.

"Enjoy growing up more."

"Don't be as hard on yourself — you'll learn from your mistakes!"

"Take time to relax and enjoy the moments as they happen."

"Don't take life too seriously. Work hard, be honest, and always be kind. Be true to yourself, don't compare yourself to others, believe in yourself, and follow your passions. It's okay to be happy, joyful, and content with yourself."

"Enjoy life and get out there."

"Every obstacle is a growth opportunity."

"Make good choices early on."

Savoring the present and finding joy in the journey can lead to a richer, more fulfilling life.

7. Additional Insights

Some insights don't fit neatly into one category but remain valuable nonetheless. Here are a few additional words of wisdom that may resonate:

"Go to law school and then get your MBA or MPA."

"Do it sooner."

"Don't expect your boss to change."

"Break the engagement earlier."

"You're doing good, keep going!"

"A job will not love you back."

"Don't take things too personally and don't overanalyze things."

"Focus on your fitness and daily habits."

These varied insights all point toward the importance of making intentional choices, staying true to yourself, and continuously striving for growth.

The advice in this chapter reflects a wide range of experiences and insights, each offering valuable lessons for navigating life with greater confidence, balance, and fulfillment. Whether it's trusting your instincts, embracing your true self, taking risks, or simply savoring the journey, these reflections offer a roadmap to a life that is both successful and deeply satisfying. As you move forward, let these lessons guide your decisions and shape your approach to the challenges and opportunities ahead.

The insights gathered from this survey provide a valuable perspective on what motivates high-potential employees and what they need to succeed. By addressing the identified challenges and focusing on developing key skills, senior leaders can better engage and retain their top talent, ensuring a strong leadership pipeline for the future.

MAKE IT HAPPEN!

1. Cultivate a Learning Environment

High-potential employees are motivated by the opportunity to learn new skills and gain valuable experience. Senior leaders should foster a culture that promotes continuous learning and provides both formal and informal avenues for skill development.

Recommendations:

- **Invest in Training Programs:** Develop comprehensive training initiatives that focus on essential skills like strategic thinking, leadership, and communication, as identified by high-potential employees.

- **Promote Mentorship:** Create a mentorship culture by pairing experienced leaders with high-potential employees to guide and support their development.

2. Support Career Development

Career growth is a key priority for high-potential employees, who look to leadership for clear pathways and guidance. Offering structured career development plans and hands-on learning opportunities helps these employees navigate their career progression more effectively.

Recommendations:

- **Implement Career Development Plans:** Collaborate with high-potential employees to create individualized career plans that define clear steps for advancement within the organization.

- **Provide Regular Feedback:** Hold consistent feedback sessions to help employees assess their progress and identify areas for growth.

3. Address Obstacles to Growth

High-potential employees often cite obstacles like lack of time and insufficient leadership support as barriers to their professional growth. Leaders must create environments that encourage development without overwhelming employees with additional responsibilities.

Recommendations:

- Allocate Time for Development: Encourage managers to dedicate time for team members to focus on their professional growth through formal training, mentorship, or on-the-job learning.

- Foster a Supportive Leadership Culture: Train senior leaders to actively support their teams by providing guidance and removing roadblocks to professional development.

Senior leaders should prioritize creating an environment that promotes continuous learning, offers clear career progression, and fosters a culture of mentorship. Doing so will help retain and develop high-potential employees, ensuring a strong leadership pipeline for the future.

For more valuable tips, visit YouNextNow.com!

CHAPTER FOURTEEN

SENIOR LEADER'S INSIGHTS
On Future Talent Needs

This chapter highlights the key results from a comprehensive survey conducted among senior leaders to better understand their concerns, challenges, and priorities related to future leadership. The study pinpoints the critical skills and attributes that senior leaders believe are essential for future success and offers actionable insights for organizations looking to strengthen their talent pipelines.

Key Findings

- Major challenges include finding the right talent, training next-level leaders, and resistance to leadership change.
- Most valued skills for future leaders are strategic thinking, problem-solving, emotional intelligence, and adaptability.
- Preferred hiring sources include internal referrals and online job postings.

You Next

This survey offers valuable insights for organizations seeking to better prepare their future leaders. By analyzing these findings, organizations can align their talent development strategies with the expectations of senior leaders, ensuring a seamless leadership transition and stronger pipelines for the future.

Survey Methodology

To deeply understand what senior leaders prioritize in future talent, a survey was conducted with 157 senior leaders, yielding an impressive 89% completion rate. Respondents represented a variety of industries and held a range of executive and management positions.

The survey focused on several key areas:

- Concerns about future leadership
- Challenges in succession planning
- Skills needed for future leaders
- Preferred hiring sources
- Attributes of the ideal hire

This data serves as a critical resource that organizations can leverage to align their leadership development strategies with the current expectations and concerns of senior leaders.

Key Findings

1. Concerns About Future Leadership

Senior leaders expressed substantial concerns regarding leadership development.

Top concern: The most pressing issue, cited by 36% of respondents, was finding the right talent.

Chapter Fourteen: Senior Leader's Insight Our Future Talent Needs

Other concerns: The next major issue was insufficient time to train next-level leaders (19%), followed by the reluctance of current leaders to step aside and allow emerging leaders the opportunity to lead (17%).

Graph 1: Top Concerns About Future Leadership

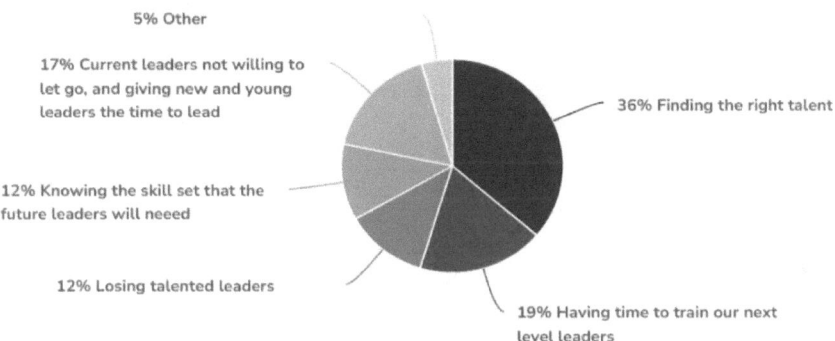

Value	Percent	Responses
Finding the right talent	36.3%	57
Having time to train our next level leaders	18.5%	29
Losing talented leaders	12.1%	19
Knowing the skill set that the future leaders will neeed	11.5%	18
Current leaders not willing to let go, and giving new and young leaders the time to lead	17.2%	27
Other	4.5%	7
		Totals: 157

2. Challenges in Succession Planning

When asked about the difficulties they encounter in succession planning, 67% of senior leaders identified finding the right talent as the primary challenge. Other notable obstacles include ensuring the right personality fit (51%) and navigating uncertainty about the specific skills that will be necessary for the future (23%).

Graph 2: Challenges in Succession Planning

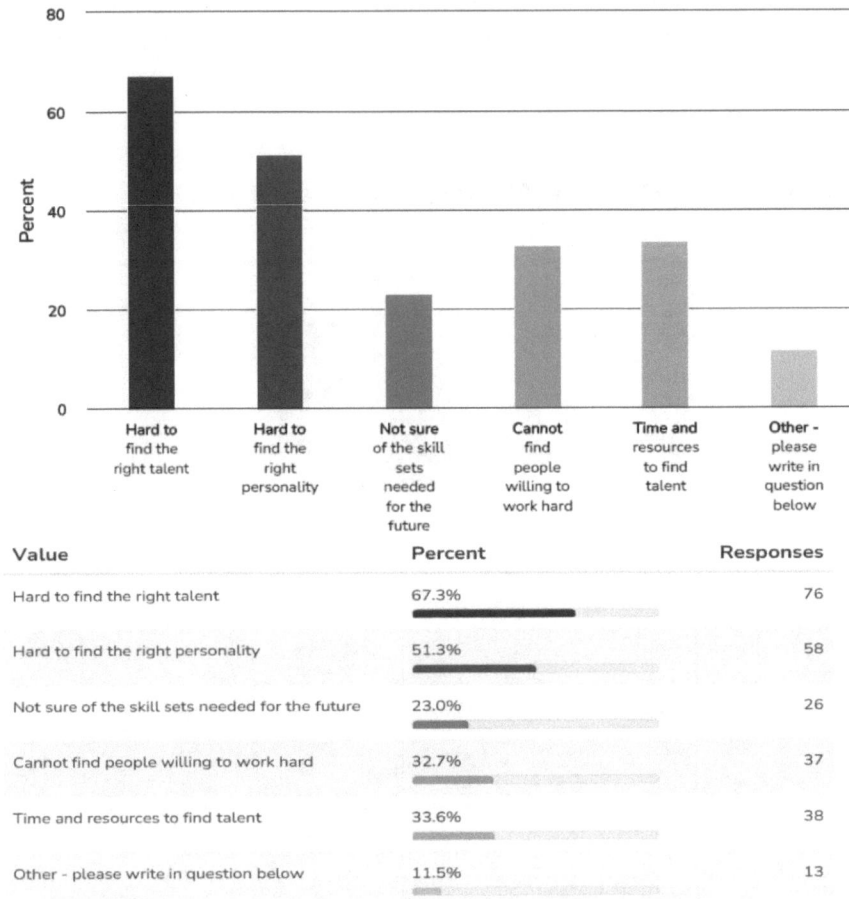

Value	Percent	Responses
Hard to find the right talent	67.3%	76
Hard to find the right personality	51.3%	58
Not sure of the skill sets needed for the future	23.0%	26
Cannot find people willing to work hard	32.7%	37
Time and resources to find talent	33.6%	38
Other - please write in question below	11.5%	13

3. Essential Skills for Future Leaders

Senior leaders were also asked to pinpoint the skills they consider crucial for future leaders. The top competencies identified include:

- Strategic Thinking: Highlighted by 83% of respondents as a critical skill for future leadership.
- Problem-Solving: Considered essential by 82% of senior leaders.
- Emotional Intelligence: Valued by 79% of respondents as key to effective leadership.

Chapter Fourteen: Senior Leader's Insight Our Future Talent Needs

- Adaptability and Flexibility: Emphasized by 85% of leaders as crucial for navigating changing circumstances.

Graph 3: Skill Sets Needed for Future Leaders

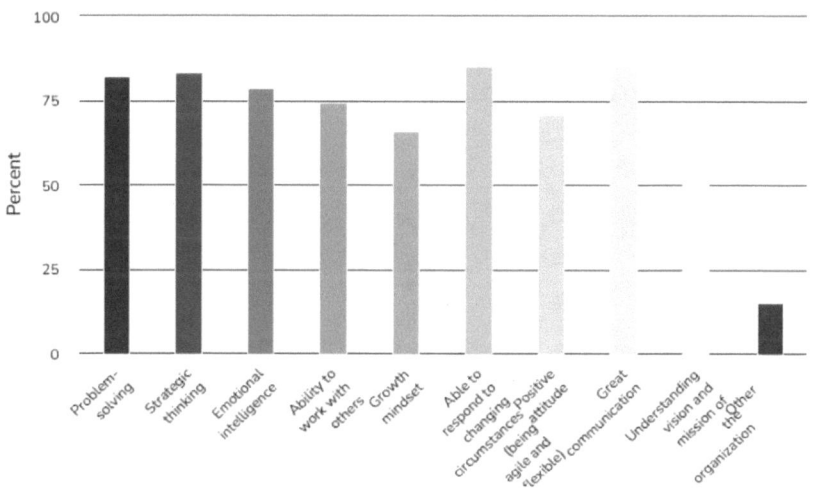

Value	Percent	Responses
Problem-solving	82.2%	129
Strategic thinking	83.4%	131
Emotional intelligence	79.0%	124
Ability to work with others	74.5%	117
Growth mindset	66.2%	104
Able to respond to changing circumstances (being agile and flexible)	85.4%	134
Positive attitude	70.7%	111
Great communication	85.4%	134
Understanding vision and mission of the organization	67.5%	106
Other - if other go to option below and write in answer	15.3%	24

4. Sources for New Hires

Senior leaders primarily rely on internal referrals (80%) and online job postings (74%) as their preferred methods for sourcing new talent. Additionally, LinkedIn is a popular recruitment platform, with 64% of respondents utilizing it for hiring.

Graph 4: Preferred Sources for New Hires

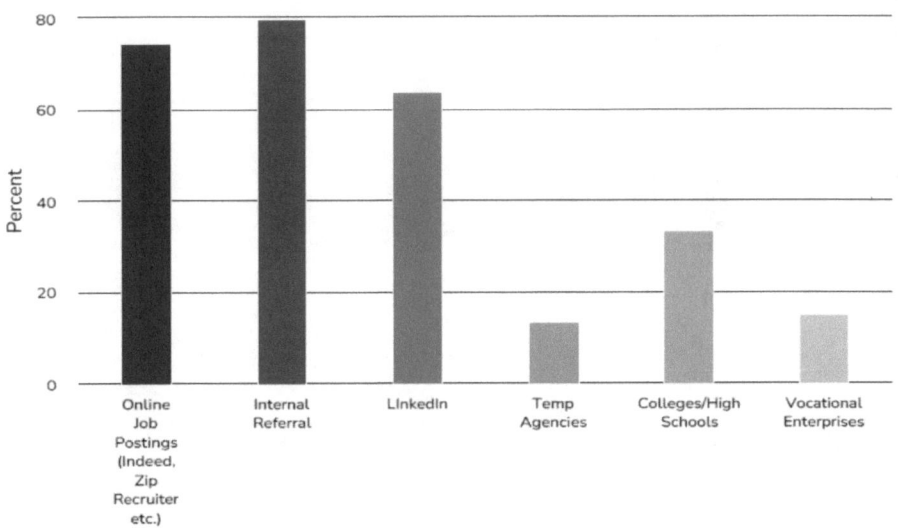

Value	Percent	Responses
Online Job Postings (Indeed, Zip Recruiter etc.)	74.3%	84
Internal Referral	79.6%	90
LinkedIn	63.7%	72
Temp Agencies	13.3%	15
Colleges/High Schools	33.6%	38
Vocational Enterprises	15.0%	17

Chapter Fourteen: Senior Leader's Insight Our Future Talent Needs

5. Attributes of the Ideal New Hire

Senior leaders described their ideal new hire as someone capable of handling multiple priorities, thriving under pressure, and adapting to dynamic environments. Additionally, effective communication and collaboration with diverse teams were deemed crucial attributes.

What Senior Leaders Want from Employees: Now and in the Future

We also conducted research that explored senior leaders' expectations for their current and future workforce. Leaders were asked to articulate what they truly need from their employees, particularly top performers. Their responses provide valuable insights into the evolving demands of the workplace, offering a clear perspective on the competencies required for both present success and future growth.

Not surprisingly, senior leaders expect more than just satisfactory job performance from their employees. They emphasize a combination of technical expertise, interpersonal skills, and leadership qualities that are essential for excelling in current roles and paving the way for future success.

Below are the key competencies prioritized by senior leaders, based on direct survey responses, along with their mostly unedited comments. Understanding these expectations can help employees align with organizational goals and maximize their contributions.

Top Skills and Attributes Desired by Senior Leaders

Unsurprisingly, senior leaders highlighted the following as the most critical skills and attributes employees should possess:

- **Problem-Solving (82%):** Leaders frequently stress the importance of employees being able to identify challenges, analyze them thoroughly, and develop practical solutions. This skill is essential for navigating today's increasingly complex business environment.

- Strategic Thinking (83%): Employees who think strategically—who see the broader picture and make decisions aligned with long-term goals—are highly valued. Strategic thinkers enable organizations to remain competitive and forward-looking.

- Emotional Intelligence (79%): The ability to understand and manage both personal emotions and those of others is key to leadership, teamwork, and effective communication. Many leaders specifically highlighted the need for empathy in the workplace.

- Collaboration (75%): Working well with diverse teams is critical in modern workplaces. Employees who excel at collaboration contribute significantly to the organization's success.

- Growth Mindset (66%): Senior leaders look for employees who are eager to learn, take on new challenges, and continually seek self-improvement. A growth mindset is essential for navigating change and driving personal and organizational progress.

- Agility and Flexibility (85%): The ability to adapt quickly to changing circumstances is more crucial than ever. Employees must demonstrate agility to effectively respond to new challenges and seize emerging opportunities.

- Positive Attitude (71%): Leaders value employees who bring optimism and enthusiasm to their work. A positive attitude enhances team morale and fosters a productive work environment.

- Great Communication (85%): Effective communication is indispensable in any role. Employees who articulate their ideas clearly, listen actively, and foster open dialogue are highly sought after.

- **Understanding the Organization's Vision and Mission (68%):** Employees who grasp and align themselves with the organization's vision and mission are more likely to make meaningful contributions to its long-term success.

By recognizing and developing these competencies, employees can position themselves for success and play a pivotal role in driving their organizations forward.

Additional Skills and Attributes Categorized

In addition to the core skills identified, senior leaders highlighted several other important attributes for employees. These qualities, derived from direct leader responses, have been categorized to provide a clearer understanding of their expectations.

Adaptability and Flexibility

- **Adaptability:** Leaders emphasize the need for employees who can "recognize and adapt to change" in dynamic environments.
- **Extreme Flexibility:** The ability to handle unpredictable situations is valued, with leaders seeking employees who demonstrate "extreme flexibility" and a "seat of your pants gambler" mentality.
- **Handling Chaos:** Employees must be able to "handle chaos" and remain productive under pressure.
- **Agility:** Quick decision-making without falling into "analysis paralysis" is essential for success in fast-moving environments.
- **Willingness to Work Beyond 9-5:** Flexibility in work hours is important, with employees being "willing to work beyond '9-5'" when necessary to meet critical deadlines.

Leadership and Influence

- Influence and Inspiration: Leaders expect employees to have the "ability to influence, impact, and inspire others."
- Accountability: Ensuring personal and team accountability is crucial for achieving results.
- Developing Others: Employees who can "develop skills in others" and focus on "intentionally developing replacement leaders from day one" are highly valued.
- Grit and Wisdom: Leaders seek individuals who exhibit "grit and wisdom" when facing challenges.
- Motivating the Next Generation: Employees who can "motivate the next generation of workers" play a vital role in sustaining organizational success.
- Delegation and Expertise: Effective leadership includes "delegation, emotional intelligence, and subject matter expertise."

Technical and Digital Skills

- Digital Transformation Expertise: With the rise of technology, leaders prioritize "digital transformation expertise" and understanding of new technologies such as AI.
- Technical Skills: Employees must possess "technical skills to work in a more automated space."
- Digital and Data Acumen: Leaders expect proficiency in "digital and data acumen" to leverage insights for decision-making.
- Embracing AI: Willingness to "embrace AI" is critical for staying competitive.

Chapter Fourteen: Senior Leader's Insight Our Future Talent Needs

Interpersonal Skills

- Listening and Inclusivity: Leaders appreciate employees who are "listening and flexible with an inclusive approach" to foster collaboration.
- Empathy: A recurring theme, "empathy" is crucial for teamwork, leadership, and decision-making.
- Conflict Resolution: The ability to "navigate conflicts" and "build cohesive teams" while transforming disengagement into commitment is highly valued.
- Effective Communication: Leaders stress the importance of "effective communication," where employees not only listen but also clearly convey their ideas.

Cultural and Organizational Fit

- Cultural Fit: Employees who align with the "cultural fit of the organization" are more likely to thrive and contribute effectively.
- Global Perspective: In a globalized world, leaders value employees with a "global perspective" for navigating international markets.
- Technology Awareness: Understanding "how technology will impact the workforce" is crucial for future leaders.

Creativity and Innovation

- Creativity: Leaders look for employees who "think outside the box" and bring "creative talent" to their roles.
- Forward-Thinking: Employees should be "forward-thinking and innovative" to drive organizational progress.
- Critical Thinking: Leaders value employees with "critical thinking skills" to challenge assumptions and promote thoughtful analysis.

You Next

- Creative Problem-Solving: The ability to "address complex system issues simply and succinctly" is critical for effective problem-solving.

Accountability and Integrity

- Moral Courage: Leaders emphasize the importance of "moral courage to challenge higher-ups" and demonstrate integrity in decision-making.
- Personal and Organizational Integrity: Maintaining both "personal and organizational integrity" is a fundamental expectation.
- Responsibility: Employees must show a "willingness to take responsibility" and "put in the time and work to gain necessary leadership skills."
- Integrity and Empathy: A combination of "integrity, adaptability, and empathy" is essential for ethical leadership.

Customer Focus and Service Orientation

- Customer Focus: Leaders prioritize employees with a strong focus on "attention to detail" and "superior service skills."
- Industry Knowledge: Employees need a deep understanding of "industry knowledge" and "domain skills" in areas like marketing or technology to remain competitive.
- Resilience and Emotional Stability
- Resilience: The ability to "overcome failure" and demonstrate "resilience, emotional regulation, and assertiveness" is critical for maintaining performance under pressure.
- Emotional Regulation: Employees must be able to "manage highly stressful situations" while maintaining positive well-being.

Coaching and Mentorship

- Mentorship: Leaders value employees who have the "ability to mentor and train" others, ensuring knowledge transfer and team development.

- Openness to Coaching: Employees who are "willing to learn and accept coaching" demonstrate the commitment to personal and professional growth.

- Innovation and Forward Thinking

- Foresight: Employees who possess "foresight, authenticity, and an inclusive mindset" are key to anticipating and navigating future trends.

- Curiosity and Questioning: The ability to "stay curious and ask thought-provoking questions" fosters innovation and forward-thinking approaches to problem-solving.

Miscellaneous Attributes

- Physical and Mental Wellness: Leaders value employees who prioritize "physical and mental wellness" to manage stress and ensure sustainable performance.

- By understanding and embodying these skills and attributes, employees can not only meet but exceed the expectations of senior leaders, positioning themselves for long-term success within their organizations.

- Humility: Senior leaders identify humility as a core trait that fosters a positive work environment and leads to more effective leadership. Humble employees tend to listen well, acknowledge their mistakes, and collaborate more effectively, promoting a culture of continuous learning.

- Courage: "Professional courage" is highly valued for its role in guiding tough decision-making and facing difficult situations head-on. It enables leaders to challenge the status quo, take calculated risks, and stand by their convictions, even in the face of adversity.

- Putting Others First: Leaders also emphasize the importance of selflessness, with a "willingness to put others' needs first" seen as a reflection of empathy and strong teamwork. This attribute helps create a supportive and cohesive team dynamic.

Accountability and Attention to Detail

- Accountability in Self and Others: The ability to "hold oneself and others accountable" is seen as essential for ensuring team success and maintaining integrity. Leaders value employees who take responsibility for their actions and results, ensuring that high standards are met consistently.

- Attention to Detail: Senior leaders appreciate employees who are "detail-oriented," ensuring that tasks are completed thoroughly and accurately. This level of diligence often translates into "superior service skills" and greater client satisfaction.

Balancing Needs and Embracing Feedback

- Balancing Organizational and Employee Needs: Leaders admire employees who can effectively "balance the needs of the employee with the needs of the company." This ability indicates strong problem-solving skills and a deeper understanding of both team dynamics and business goals.

- Willingness to Learn and Accept Coaching: Continuous learning is key to professional growth. Leaders want employees who demonstrate a "willingness to help train others to be leaders," contributing to a culture of mentorship and development within the organization.

Chapter Fourteen: Senior Leader's Insight Our Future Talent Needs

Foresight and Wellness

- Foresight and Authenticity: Leaders expect employees to bring "foresight" to their roles, helping the organization anticipate trends and challenges. Authenticity, combined with an "inclusive mindset," strengthens trust within teams and ensures a more engaged workforce.

- Physical and Mental Wellness: Leaders highly value employees who prioritize their "physical and mental wellness." Maintaining a balanced state of physical, mental, spiritual, and emotional well-being not only enhances leadership effectiveness but also promotes sustainability in performance over the long term.

Training and Mentorship

- Training and Mentorship: Leaders place great importance on mentorship, expecting employees to be "willing to help train others to be leaders." This focus on leadership development is critical for nurturing the next generation of leaders, ensuring organizational longevity and adaptability.

Senior leaders have outlined a comprehensive vision for the skills and attributes they value most in employees, ranging from technical proficiency (problem-solving, strategic thinking) to interpersonal strengths (emotional intelligence, effective communication). As the workplace evolves, these skills will continue to be crucial for employees looking to grow and excel in their careers.

Understanding these expectations enables employees to align themselves with organizational goals, enhancing both personal growth and contributing to the overall success of their organizations. By cultivating the identified skills and addressing challenges in succession planning, organizations can ensure a well-prepared leadership pipeline for the future.

References

The insights and findings presented in this chapter are drawn from a proprietary survey conducted among senior leaders from 37 industries. For further insights, literature on leadership development, succession planning, and talent management may be referenced to support these recommendations.

MAKE IT HAPPEN!

1. Address the Leadership Gap

The survey revealed that 36% of senior leaders are concerned about finding the right talent for future leadership roles. This concern is further complicated by the challenge of training new leaders within limited timeframes. To bridge this gap, organizations must adopt a proactive approach to leadership development, focusing on identifying high-potential employees early and providing them with the resources they need to grow.

Recommendations:

- Talent Identification Programs: Implement formal programs to identify high-potential leaders within the organization.
- Leadership Development Initiatives: Invest in targeted leadership development programs that focus on essential skills like strategic thinking, problem-solving, and emotional intelligence.

2. Overcome Challenges in Succession Planning

With 67% of senior leaders identifying talent acquisition as a major challenge in succession planning, organizations need to refine their approaches to both talent development and hiring. The difficulty in finding individuals with the right personality fit suggests that organizations must consider cultural alignment alongside technical skills during the hiring process.

Recommendations:

- Integrated Succession Planning: Develop a succession planning strategy that aligns talent acquisition with leadership development efforts.
- Cultural Fit Assessments: Incorporate cultural fit assessments into the hiring process to ensure long-term success.

3. Emphasize Essential Leadership Skills

The survey data highlights the importance of certain key leadership skills:

- Strategic thinking (83%)
- Problem-solving (82%)
- Emotional intelligence (79%)
- Adaptability and flexibility (85%)

These skills are essential for navigating an increasingly dynamic business environment, underscoring the need for leadership training to focus on these competencies.

Recommendations:

- Skill-Focused Training Programs: Design training programs to prioritize these essential skills.
- Emotional Intelligence Development: Offer coaching or workshops aimed at building emotional intelligence, particularly in areas such as empathy, self-awareness, and communication.

4. Leverage Preferred Hiring Sources

Senior leaders favor internal referrals (80%) and online job postings (74%) for new hires, with LinkedIn (64%) also playing a prominent role. These preferences underscore the need to maintain strong internal recruitment channels while exploring innovative hiring strategies.

Recommendations:

- Strengthening Referral Programs: Encourage employee participation in referral programs by offering incentives and recognizing successful referrals.
- Enhancing Online Presence: Optimize job postings and leverage LinkedIn profiles to attract a wider, more diverse candidate pool.

5. Prepare Ideal New Hires for Success

The ideal new hire, as described by senior leaders, can handle multiple priorities, work under pressure, and adapt to changing environments. These attributes are vital in a fast-paced and complex workplace where leaders must manage uncertainty effectively.

Recommendations:

- Onboarding Programs: Develop onboarding programs that help new hires quickly integrate into the company's culture and align with its expectations.

- Continuous Learning Opportunities: Offer ongoing professional development to build adaptability, resilience, and communication skills over time.

Organizations should focus on enhancing these critical leadership skills in their development programs and address the identified challenges through targeted succession planning strategies.

Download the full white paper at YouNextNow.com.

APPENDIX

Appendix A

"State of the Job" Assessment

- How long have you been with the organization?
- How long have you been in your current role?
- What were your expectations when you first moved into that position?
- What about your role has changed and what has stayed the same over the past 12 months?
- What are the three best things about your current job?
- What are the three worst things about your current job?
- Do you like the organization but don't feel like your current role is a good fit?
- Do you like your current job but don't feel like the organization is a good fit?
- How well does your existing team work together?
- Do you get along well with your current supervisor?
- If you could make a change, what would that look like?
- Are there realistic opportunities for advancement within your current organization?

Appendix B

Your Career Assets Worksheet

TALENTS

What are your natural gifts?

NOTES

SKILLS

What abilities have you gained and practiced in an effort to improve and advance?

NOTES

You Next

EDUCATION

What learning opportunities have you pursued?

_____

_____

NOTES

EXPERIENCE

How much time have you spent applying your career assets in real-world situations?

_____

_____

NOTES

You Next

Appendix C

Your Values Exercise

One way to help define your values is to look at this process through the corporate lens. Businesses often go through the same exercise. Here are a few well-known examples:

Southwest Airlines
Values: Friendly, Respectful, Passionate, Customer-Focused, Fun

Airbnb
Values: Caring, Adventurous, Hospitable, Resourceful, Flexible

Apple
Values: Innovative, Collaborative, Enthusiastic, Ambitious, Bold

Take note: Not a single mention of transportation, lodging, or computers! It's all about the "flavor" these brands want to project to the world and to their customers.

My family and friends say they appreciate that I am _____

_____

My co-workers say they can always count on me to be ____

_____

I'm proud that I am _____

Circle the values that apply to you.

Accepting	Appreciative	Careful
Adaptable	Attentive	Collaborative

You Next

Committed	Fearless	Persuasive
Compassionate	Flexible	Purposeful
Concerned	Friendly	Reliable
Considerate	Generous	Resilient
Consistent	Grateful	Resourceful
Cooperative	Hard-Working	Respectful
Creative	Honest	Responsible
Decisive	Humble	Sincere
Dependable	Joyful	Tactful
Determined	Kind	Team-Oriented
Diligent	Loving	Trustworthy
Discerning	Loyal	Truthful
Effective	Optimistic	Understanding
Enthusiastic	Patient	Unshakable
Fair	Persistent	Upbeat

If you've circled quite a few value words, you might find it helpful to narrow down the list to your top 3-5 choices.

You Next

Appendix D

Gap Map Resources

Sample Gap Map

	TODAY: Junior Manager	VISION: CEO
Talents/ Skills	Finance, Operations	Business, Operations, Communications
Emotional Intelligence	Average	Very High
Education	Bachelor's Degree in Finance	MBA, Continuing Education, Industry Certifications
Experience(s)	Bank Teller, Junior Manager	Multiple Organizations/Departments/Roles, Progressive Leadership Responsibilities; Successful Coach/Mentor; Past President of Industry Association; Board of Directors for a Local Nonprofit; Community Involvement; Well-Connected.
Values/ Reputation	Hard-Working, Dependable, Kind	Driven, Decisive, Enthusiastic

Appendix

Your Gap Map

	TODAY:	VISION:
Talents/ Skills		
Emotional Intelligence		
Education		
Experience(s)		
Values/ Reputation		

Your Targeted Gap Fillers

	TODAY:	VISION:
Talents/ Skills		
Emotional Intelligence		
Education		
Experience(s)		
Values/ Reputation		

Appendix E

Action Plan

Things You Can Do Starting Today

	TODAY:	VISION:
Talents/ Skills		
Emotional Intelligence		
Education		
Experience(s)		
Values/ Reputation		

Things You Can Do Within the Next 12 Months

	TODAY:	VISION:
Talents/ Skills		
Emotional Intelligence		
Education		
Experience(s)		
Values/ Reputation		

You Next

Things You can Do Within the Next Five Years

	TODAY:	VISION:
Talents/Skills		
Emotional Intelligence		
Education		
Experience(s)		
Values/Reputation		

Appendix F

Credibility Gut Check Worksheet

Use this worksheet to do a gut check on how credible your peers consider you to be.

1. **Do your colleagues and co-workers see you as someone they can count on?**

	YES	NO
• Are you consistent in your actions and decisions?	☐	☐
• Do you follow through on commitments, regardless of the difficulty or inconvenience?	☐	☐

2. **Do you keep your promises?**

	YES	NO
• Do you often deliver on the commitments you make to your team	☐	☐
• Are you known for meeting deadlines and honoring agreements?	☐	☐

3. **Do you live every day according to your values and morals?**

	YES	NO
• Are your actions aligned with the ethical standards you profess to uphold?	☐	☐
• Do you make decisions based on what is right, rather than what is easy or advantageous?	☐	☐

4. Do you get a little fast and loose with the truth when it suits your needs?

                                                                   YES   NO

- Do you ever compromise your integrity to achieve short-term goals? ☐ ☐
- Are there situations where you justify bending the truth for personal gain? ☐ ☐

5. How do you handle mistakes?

                                                                   YES   NO

- Do you take responsibility for your errors, or do you look for ways to deflect blame? ☐ ☐
- Are you transparent about your mistakes and proactive in finding solutions? ☐ ☐

6. How do you respond to feedback?

                                                                   YES   NO

- Are you open to constructive criticism and willing to make necessary changes? ☐ ☐
- Do you actively seek feedback from your peers to improve your performance? ☐ ☐

7. Are you reliable in your communication?

                                                                   YES   NO

- Do you communicate openly and honestly with your team? ☐ ☐

Appendix

- Are you timely in providing updates and responding to inquiries?

8. **How do you support your team members?**

                                                                                           YES   NO

   - Do you offer help and support to colleagues when they need it?
   - Are you willing to go the extra mile to ensure team success?

9. **Do you respect confidentiality?**

                                                                                           YES   NO

   - Can your team trust you with sensitive information?
   - Do you honor the privacy of your colleagues and maintain professional discretion?

10. **Are you consistent in your behavior?**

                                                                                            YES   NO

    - Do you maintain the same ethical standards and behavior, regardless of who is watching?
    - Are you a steady and dependable presence in the workplace?

11. How do you handle conflicts?

	YES	NO
• Do you address conflicts with fairness and a focus on resolution?		
• Are you seen as a mediator who can be trusted to handle disputes impartially?		

12. Do you demonstrate empathy and understanding?

	YES	NO
• Are you considerate of your colleagues' feelings and perspectives?		
• Do you show genuine concern for the well-being of others?		

Appendix G

Mentorship Questions

1. How do you stay updated with industry trends and continue learning?
2. What networking advice would you offer?
3. Can you recommend any books, podcasts, or resources that have been particularly helpful lately?
4. What aspects of your career are you most passionate about, and why?
5. What skills are you currently focusing on developing?
6. Have there been any recent projects or tasks where you felt really challenged?
7. How do you organize and prioritize your workload?
8. What are you grateful for this week?
9. What are you proud of this week?
10. What are you struggling with this week?
11. How do you handle setbacks and failures in your career?
12. What strategies do you use to maintain work-life balance?
13. How do you approach decision-making in complex situations?
14. What role does mentorship play in your own professional growth?
15. How do you stay motivated during tough times?
16. What advice do you have for setting and achieving long-term career goals?
17. Can you share an example of a difficult decision you had to make and how you handled it?
18. What are the key qualities you believe are essential for leadership?

19. How do you handle and give constructive feedback?
20. What are some effective ways to manage stress and avoid burnout?
21. How do you foster innovation and creativity within your team?
22. What are the biggest changes you've seen in the industry, and how have you adapted to them?
23. How do you measure success in your role?
24. What's one piece of advice you wish you had received early in your career?
25. How do you ensure that you're continuously improving in your role?
26. What are your favorite techniques for problem-solving?
27. How do you build and maintain strong professional relationships?
28. What are some common mistakes you see professionals making, and how can they be avoided?
29. How do you balance short-term tasks with long-term objectives?
30. What impact do you hope to have on your organization and industry?

These questions are designed to facilitate deep and meaningful conversations, providing both the mentor and mentee with valuable insights and growth opportunities. Regularly addressing these questions can help ensure that the mentorship relationship is mutually beneficial and continuously evolving.

You Next

Appendix H

Workbook Excerpt

Have you ever been frustrated with yourself because you can't seem to get things done?

Do you ever find yourself avoiding meaningful tasks that you know you need or want to do?

Have you ever filled your time with unproductive activities, only to create stress for yourself later?

This is procrastination. And we all do it.

Procrastination is the act of avoiding what you need to do by distracting yourself with other tasks until you're up against a deadline.

It might feel like a hidden habit, one you prefer to keep to yourself. But the truth is, far more people struggle with procrastination than you might realize.

> **This interactive workbook is designed to get you thinking about:**
> - How much you procrastinate
> - What triggers procrastination
> - What behaviors to change
> - How to become more proactive

And of course, it's designed to help you work though it and take action to leave procrastination behind.

Appendix

Everyone Procrastinates

Procrastination affects us all, yet some conquer it while others suffer its consequences. This behavior is often a way to avoid tasks, usually triggered by feeling overwhelmed or overthinking.

Chronic procrastination can lead to missed opportunities, increased stress, and serious personal or professional problems. It heightens the risk of missing deadlines, undervaluing others' time, being unprepared, or relying on others more than necessary.

Overcoming procrastination is key to success. It builds confidence, enhances your reputation, and saves time and money.

Proactive individuals enjoy both spontaneity and reliability. By managing time effectively, you can seize opportunities and avoid disappointment. Breaking the cycle of procrastination unlocks powerful habits and helps you reach your goals. Tackling your to-do list can mean the difference between having time for something unexpected and fun or having to say no because of looming deadlines. While procrastination may feel like buying extra time, it usually ends up costing you more.

This interactive guide will help you identify your triggers and behaviors, equipping you to become more proactive. Explore your personal habits and create action plans to overcome procrastination, reducing stress and boosting productivity.

> Don't procrastinate on going through this material! Give yourself the time to dive in and create a distraction-free environment to fully absorb the information. Block out time on your calendar, pour your favorite drink, and have a pen or device ready to jot down notes and work through the exercises. This will help you take the first steps toward making proactive changes and overcoming procrastination.

You Next

Check List

Ask Yourself

Let's go through the different ways in which you could be procrastinating.

Check every box that resonates with you.

- ☐ I frequently delay tasks I know need to be done
- ☐ I often feel overwhelmed when faced with tasks
- ☐ I have missed deadlines or important opportunities due to procrastination
- ☐ I struggle to maintain a proactive mindset in my daily life
- ☐ I recognize the triggers that lead me to procrastinate
- ☐ I have developed proactive plans to overcome procrastination
- ☐ I experience stress, anxiety, guilt, or shame due to procrastination
- ☐ I have noticed a negative impact on my personal or professional reputation due to procrastination
- ☐ I have missed out on spontaneous opportunities due to poor time management
- ☐ I am actively seeking ways to combat procrastination and develop productive habits

PART I

CAN WE PUT OFF PROCRASTINATION?

Procrastination is a widespread issue, affecting roughly 20 percent of people at any given moment. It's crucial to distinguish procrastination from laziness. Unlike laziness, where minimal effort is expended, procrastinators often put significant energy into avoiding tasks until the last possible moment.

Contrary to what some may think, procrastination is far from effortless. It takes a serious emotional toll, often leading to stress-related behaviors such as sleep disruption, overeating or undereating, anxiety, and analysis paralysis. Over time, it can also foster feelings of shame, fear, and even physical symptoms like headaches.

In truth, the idea of working better under pressure is a myth. The skills needed to produce quality work are always there but often stay dormant until deadlines approach. Overcoming procrastination means developing the discipline to access those abilities consistently, rather than depending on the adrenaline of last-minute efforts. By fostering self-discipline, individuals can unlock their full potential and maintain steady productivity, leading to higher-quality results and reduced stress.

> Procrastinators are not indifferent; they are fully aware of the impact their delays have on themselves and others. Despite the common claim that they "perform better under pressure," procrastination actually hinders the full realization of their potential. The brief surge of productivity that occurs under tight deadlines highlights not a special ability to thrive under stress, but rather a lack of discipline and effective time management. This pattern can prevent individuals from achieving their best work and leaves untapped potential on the table.

You Next

PART II

WORKSHEET
Productivity

DATE _____

CALLS TO MAKE

Phone # or Person	Regarding

FOLLOW-UP

Appointments/Meetings

Time	Person/Place

To-Do

Today's Accomplishments

_____

_____

PART III

WHEN SAYING YES CREATES PROCRASTINATION

One of the main triggers for procrastination is the perception of not having enough time to complete tasks, which is often linked to overcommitment. Overcommitting—whether actively agreeing to take on more tasks or passively accumulating responsibilities—can lead to stress and ultimately result in procrastination. It's important to realize that excessive agreeability, driven by fear of missing out (FOMO), the desire to please others, or a sense of obligation, can undermine your ability to meet commitments.

Constantly saying yes stretches your capacity to manage time effectively and accomplish tasks efficiently. This, in turn, can create delays and lead to more procrastination. To break this cycle, you must protect your time and set boundaries. Prioritizing tasks based on their importance and urgency helps streamline commitments, while practicing the art of saying no—even in situations where it may feel awkward—is essential for avoiding overcommitment and maintaining balance.

Learning to say no allows you to manage your workload better, reduce stress, and maintain focus on the tasks that truly matter.

Ultimately, overcoming procrastination requires a fundamental shift in mindset. It involves recognizing the importance of setting clear boundaries, confidently saying no when necessary, and consistently prioritizing tasks based on their importance and alignment with personal or professional goals.

Proactive individuals understand the value of self-imposed limits and how they contribute to more effective task management. By being intentional with their time and energy, they prevent overwhelming commitments from piling up, which in turn reduces stress. This shift toward intentional action allows for better productivity, stronger decision-making, and a more balanced life. Taking control of your time and priorities helps to break the cycle of procrastination and fosters a mindset geared toward long-term success and personal growth.

> Shifting from an obligation-driven mindset to a priority-focused approach is a powerful way to combat procrastination. When you say yes out of obligation rather than genuine desire or alignment with your goals, it often leads to feelings of resentment, stress, and ultimately, delays in completing tasks. This misalignment between your commitments and true priorities creates cognitive dissonance, which can further fuel procrastination.
>
> By consciously aligning your actions with what matters most to you, you not only reduce the emotional conflict but also enhance your overall productivity. This shift helps you focus on meaningful tasks, manage your time more effectively, and increase your sense of accomplishment. Prioritizing your commitments ensures that you're working toward your goals, rather than just fulfilling obligations, which leads to more fulfillment and less procrastination.

Appendix

PROTECT YOUR TIME

It's okay to say you don't have the time to do the job with the attention it deserves. Nice phrases to protect your time are:

> "I will have the ability to start that project at the beginning of the third quarter."

> "As long as you are okay with receiving that in a week, I can manage that."

> "My schedule is 100 percent full right now."

> "Someone else might be able to devote more time to this."

> "I don't foresee having the bandwidth to handle this project."

> "No. Thanks for asking me to be included. Now is not a good time for me to take on any more responsibilities."

Appendix I

Effective Phrases for Leaders

Powerful Phrases	Demonstrates
I'm sorry.	Awareness & responsibility
Tell me more about what you are thinking.	Interest & listening skills
I'm proud of what you accomplished.	Individual & team accomplishments
What is working well for you?	Positive focus
How can I help?	Help & caring
What are your goals?	Concern for person & team
What do you think people are concerned about?	Trusts others' opinions
You have my full support.	Confidence & trust
I'm proud to work with you because…	Appreciation & teamwork
What can I do to make your role easier?	Confidence & trust
Is there something you want to discuss?	Empathy & caring
How can we improve our part of the organization?	Confidence & trust
What are our customers saying?	Awareness & concern
What else should we be thinking about?	Interest & trust
Because we are better than that.	Setting high expectations
You are right.	Validation & trust
That is a great point.	Validation & appreciation
I trust you to make the right decision.	Trust & confidence

Appendix J

Ask for a Promotion Checklist

The Checklist: Ask for a Promotion

1. *Assess your developmental readiness:*
   - ☐ Do you have the proper skills and talents for a higher position?
   - ☐ Do you have the necessary education and certifications?
   - ☐ Do you have the right experience?
   - ☐ Have you made it clear to your supervisor that you are committed to the organization and want to advance?
   - ☐ Have you asked for constructive feedback and made improvements?

2. *Know the proper procedures for moving up within your company:*
   - ☐ Do you know exactly who to ask for a promotion?
   - ☐ What other people will be involved in making the decision?
   - ☐ Have you met the criteria and performed at a superior level that would warrant asking for a promotion?
   - ☐ Have you documented and quantified your success?
   - ☐ Have you made the decision-makers aware of your success?
   - ☐ Who are you competing with for this promotion? *(internal or external)*
   - ☐ What personnel changes would need to happen for a new position to be available?
   - ☐ Have you reviewed your request and presentation with a mentor or colleague before officially asking for the promotion?

3. **Demonstrate leadership and planning:**
   - ☐ Have you displayed your ability to lead teams and motivate employees?
   - ☐ Can you show that you have thoroughly researched the new role and responsibilities?
   - ☐ Have you prepared a factual case for your promotion, including a bulleted summary of your accomplishments? *(1-2 pages)*
   - ☐ Can you describe how your achievements have specifically added value to the company?
   - ☐ Have you shadowed or been mentored by someone in the desired position?
   - ☐ Have you been actively training your replacement?
   - ☐ Have you crafted a plan to explain what you would do during your first 90 days in the new position?

4. **Be savvy about timing:**
   - ☐ Is now the right time to ask for a promotion?
   - ☐ Are there other situations occurring that could reduce your odds of a positive response? *(recent layoffs, loss of a big contract, a personal emergency, etc.)*
   - ☐ Could you plan to ask for the promotion after being recognized for a successful effort or honored with an award?

5. **Identify what you really want from advancement:**
   - ☐ More power
   - ☐ More prestige
   - ☐ More influence

- ☐ More responsibility
- ☐ More money
- ☐ More benefits
- ☐ Other

6. *Identify the impact you want to make on your team and the organization:*
   - ☐ Develop people
   - ☐ Increase results
   - ☐ Set strategic direction
   - ☐ Advance depth of leadership
   - ☐ Grow as a leader and influencer
   - ☐ Transform the organization
   - ☐ Other

ABOUT THE AUTHORS

Meridith Elliott Powell, MBA

Business Growth, Sales and Leadership Expert

Meridith is a business strategist, keynote speaker, and award-winning author with expertise in business growth, sales, and leadership strategies. She has been recognized as "One of the Top 15 Business Growth Experts to Watch" by Currency Fair and "One of the Top 20 Sales Experts to Follow" by LinkedIn.

As a former C-suite executive, Meridith brings extensive experience from the banking, healthcare, and finance industries. She has earned numerous prestigious accreditations, including Master Certified Strategist, Executive Coach, and Certified Speaking Professional (a designation held by fewer than 12% of professional speakers), as well as Master Certified DISC Trainer and Coach, having facilitated and coached thousands in that program.

Meridith imparts her business expertise to organizations through innovative messages grounded in real-life examples and practical knowledge. She is the author of six books, including THRIVE: Strategies to Turn Uncertainty Into Competitive Advantage; Who Comes Next? Leadership Succession Planning Made Easy (Gold Medal winner: Nonfiction Authors Association); The Best Sales Book Ever! (Gold Medal winner: Nonfiction Authors Association); Winning in the Trust & Value Economy (USA Best Book Awards finalist); and Own It: Redefining Responsibility – Stories of Power, Freedom & Purpose.

Contact Meridith

Email: mere@valuespeaker.com

Office: (828) 243-3510

Toll-Free: (888) 526-9998

Follow on

Mary C. Kelly, PhD

Commander, U.S. Navy (ret)

Leadership Strategist and Economist

Mary specializes in leadership growth that enhances organizational profitability and productivity, particularly in finance, insurance, real estate, and manufacturing. A graduate of the Naval Academy, Mary served 25 years on active duty, primarily in Asia, where she led multicultural teams across nine countries. Her distinguished career included roles as an intelligence officer, chief of police, HR director, and chief of staff, along with training more than 40,000 military personnel.

Mary has also been a professor of leadership and economics at the Naval Academy, the Air Force Academy, and Hawaii Pacific University. She is the author of 20 business books, including her best-seller, Master Your World, which was named a "must-read" by MENSA and MOAA, Why Leaders Fail and the 7 Prescriptions for Success, profiled in Forbes and Success magazines, and Who Comes Next? Leadership Succession Planning Made Easy, which won the Benjamin Franklin Gold Medal from the Nonfiction Authors Association. The Five-Minute Leadership Guide and Stop Procrastinating Tomorrow are among her team's favorite books.

Mary is a Hall of Fame speaker with the National Speakers Association and a Hall of Fame Author In Colorado. As a leadership adviser collaborating with businesses, associations, and government agencies, Mary draws from her unique background and diverse experiences. She offers programs that are content-rich, highly entertaining, and strategically designed to help her clients achieve results.

Mary's team wants you to know that, in real life, she is both fun and funny, and she loves dogs.

You Next

Contact Mary

Email: mary@productiveleaders.com

Office: (719) 357-7360

Mobile: (443) 995-8663

Follow on

Made in United States
Troutdale, OR
01/21/2025